MW00397042

Praise for *Backyard Dutch Oven Cooking*

"I've known Bruce for quite a while, and we have both cooked and judged cook-offs side-by-side. He is an amazing Dutch oven chef with delicious results! His last book, *Dutch Oven Baking*, has a proud place in my collection. I learned a lot from the recipes there. In *Backyard Dutch Oven Cooking*, there is a wealth of delicious recipes with simple, clear instructions. I'm particularly excited to try the Porcupine Meatballs! Bruce is one of my favorite Dutch oven authors."

— Mark Hansen, author of *Best of the Black Pot*, *Dutch Oven Breads*, *Around the World in a Dutch Oven*, and *Black Pot for Beginners* (visit www.marksblackpot.com)

"When I became the food editor at the *Standard-Examiner* in 1993, I judged my first Dutch oven cook-off, and that's where I met Bruce and Vickie Tracy. Dutch oven cooking has a huge following in Utah, and Bruce was one of those aspiring cooks who took his culinary skills to another level every year. He became a force to be reckoned with on the highly competitive cook-off circuit.

"In 2000, I became food editor at the *Deseret News* in Salt Lake City and began judging the International Dutch Oven Society's World Championship Cook-Off. This is the Olympics of Dutch oven cooking. Just getting a berth is an achievement, since teams have to win an IDOS-sanctioned cook-off in order to qualify. The contestants pull out all the stops, with dishes that you're more likely see at a four-star restaurant.

"Bruce competed several times at the World Championship. He learned something from every experience. When he and Vickie took the title in 2004, they wowed the judges with Cheese-Stuffed Pork Loin with New Potatoes and Stuffed Mushrooms, a perfectly baked Challah Holiday Bread with Parmesan Dipping Butter, and a stunning Poached Pear and Almond Tart.

"I was one of the judges that year, along with a culinary school professor who praised the tart's technical perfection. But actually, I love the savory flavors of Bruce's Cheese Onion Rolls best of all. With this book, you can learn the secrets from the master."

— Valerie Phillips, former *Deseret News* food editor, *Standard-Examiner* food columnist, and author of *Soup's On!: 100 Soups, Stews and Chilis Made Easy* (visit www.chewandchat.com)

BACKYARD
Dutch Oven
COOKING

BRUCE TRACY

HOBBLE CREEK PRESS
AN IMPRINT OF CEDAR FORT, INC.
SPRINGVILLE, UTAH

© 2015 Bruce Tracy
Photography on pages 88, 91, and 101 courtesy of Zach Williams; used with permission.
All rights reserved.

No part of this book may be reproduced in any form whatsoever, whether by graphic, visual, electronic, film, microfilm, tape recording, or any other means, without prior written permission of the publisher, except in the case of brief passages embodied in critical reviews and articles.

ISBN 13: 978-1-4621-1420-7

Published by Hobble Creek Press, an imprint of Cedar Fort, Inc.
2373 W. 700 S., Springville, UT 84663
Distributed by Cedar Fort, Inc., www.cedarfort.com

LIBRARY OF CONGRESS CATALOGING-IN-PUBLICATION DATA

Tracy, Bruce
Backyard dutch oven cooking / Bruce Tracy.
    pages cm
Includes index.
ISBN 978-1-4621-1420-7 (alk. paper)
1. Dutch oven cooking. 2. Outdoor cooking. I. Title

TX840.D88T729 2015
641.5'89--dc23

                    2014040271

Cover design by Lauren Error
Cover design © 2015 Lyle Mortimer
Edited by Justin Greer

Printed in the United States of America

10 9 8 7 6 5 4 3 2 1

Printed on acid-free paper

To Vickie, love of my life, who stands by me at every turn.
And to every dad and grandpa who cooks the weekend dinners for their families and
friends in the backyards of America.

Contents

Preface

Over twenty years ago, my wife, Vickie, gave me a 12-inch Dutch oven for Father's Day. I read the seasoning instructions and tried it out on the family, cooking one of master cook Val Cowley's recipes. It was a huge hit. That oven is still my prime baking oven today.

Several weeks later, I saw a notice in the local daily newspaper for the Cherry Days Dutch oven cook-off in North Ogden, Utah. I said to myself, "We can do that!" That first cook-off was a giant eye-opener for us; we didn't know the first thing about proper etiquette, and although the food was delicious, we finished last. Naturally, we tried again and began to win, accumulating experience, Dutch ovens, and other outdoor cooking equipment along the way. I was hooked.

Over time, we became good enough to be invited to the World Championship Cook-off. The stories from those cook-offs could be a book by itself . . . like the time I destroyed a chocolate banana zucchini cake and Vickie acquired another zucchini from a nearby farm so we could bake another cake.

During our ten-year competition cooking career, we cooked all over Utah, Idaho, and Wyoming, winning dozens of first-place trophies and countless cast-iron prizes. I still remember when Ruth Kendrick, world winner with Janet Wayman in 1998, told me that I was a bread master. I didn't think I was that good, but we decided we could actually win the world contest if we focused on that goal. It all came together at the 2004 World Championship Cook-off, where we won the big one.

These days, we don't compete, but we teach classes and judge cook-offs at all levels, teaching new and seasoned cooks our cooking techniques and other cooking tricks learned while we were competing.

We still cook in our backyard for our extended family and the neighbors.

Remember, it's all about the family and the food!

Introduction

Buy Quality Dutch Ovens

Which Dutch oven should you buy? Buy quality, and with proper care they will last several generations. My oldest oven was my grandmother's. It was made in the 1930s. Camp Chef and Lodge are the best and I have ovens from each company.

Every backyard cook should have a 10-inch, a 12-inch, and maybe a 14-inch oven. Having these sizes allows you to prepare any Dutch oven recipe.

I also have a set of MACA ovens from Springville, Utah. They are very heavy duty and the larger ones can be used to feed crowds. Just remember: where you cook is also where you serve. My 17-inch weighs over 70 pounds—empty! It will cook 40 pounds of meat at a time. Additionally, the extra mass of these MACA ovens is real handy when you want the food to stay hot for a longer time, like at a potluck dinner.

These days, Dutch ovens arrive preseasoned. But even preseasoned ovens need a bit more seasoning. As you begin your outdoor cooking adventure, cook something greasy like a "bacon-potato-cheese something" dish a few times. When baking bread, spray first with a good nonstick cooking spray. Also, the first few times you cook in your oven, avoid high-acid foods like tomatoes. As you do this, your cast iron will begin to build a black carbon coating called the patina. A well-seasoned oven will be as nonstick as a Teflon pan.

Basic Tools

When I began cooking in these versatile pots, I cooked on a metal garbage can lid which sat on three old bricks. Of course, these days I have several cooking stands, but you really only need some metal to separate the coals from the ground. From time to time someone will tell me they put coals right on the ground to cook. That doesn't work—the ground soaks up too much of the available heat, leaving you without enough heat to cook your food.

Another thing I did before I cooked the first dish was purchase a pair of long, cheap dollar-store tongs because I saw Val Cowley using them to transfer coals at a cooking demonstration. I haven't changed that.

Everyone should get some kind of lid lifter. They come in dozens of styles. I use Camp Chef and Mair versions because they actually clamp on the lid for greater control. You will need some type of metal rack on which to place the lid when checking your food.

Here's a picture of my metal rack; it's just old horseshoes welded into a triangle shape.

A pair of heavy gloves will save your hands when you are new to this type of outdoor cooking. I use rubber gloves to prepare many dishes because cleanup is a snap, especially when you are not near a water source!

I also wipe out the pots with paper towels after a meal. This takes care of 90% of the cleanup.

Make sure you have an 8-inch chef's knife and at least one good cutting board. This will let you slice and dice anything.

You should also have several quick-release ice cream scoops of different sizes. They are invaluable for making small, round portions of food—good for meatballs and rolls and such. I use a #50, a #10, and a #8. (The number is the number of scoops in a quart.)

Parchment paper rings for cakes will make your life easier when baking cakes. Use the oven lid to draw a template on a sheet of parchment paper. Use scissors to cut one inch inside of the mark to make a circle.

When you're ready to bake a cake, spray the oven with nonstick cooking spray, add the paper disk, and spray that too (see the photo below). Carefully pour the batter into the oven. When your cake is done, simply flip the whole oven over onto a lid-holder trivet and lift the oven. It will release very easily.

The lid is now the serving platter, or you can slide it onto a serving plate. Remember to remove the paper—it's hard to cut and doesn't taste good. I try to keep several of these premade wonders on hand.

Parchment paper lifts for pies are a great way to get a pie or tart out of a Dutch oven. For a 12-inch oven, take an 18- to 20-inch sheet and cut into 3 strips. Spray the oven with nonstick cooking spray and evenly arrange the paper strips in the oven one at a time, spraying each one as you add it (see image below). This gives you six handles.

Now add the bottom crust of your pie. Before you put the lid on to bake the dish, trim the strips a little so they won't get in the way of the food. When the pie is done, use the handles to lift the pie out of the oven and place it on the lid.

I know it looks like it needs three people, but you can do it with two. If the pie is really loose, find a third person to give you a hand. After the pie cools a bit, cut one end of each lift off and pull the other end from under the pie to remove it. You could do this with any number of strips—I've seen as few as two strips and as many as twelve. Three strips (six handles) works best for me, as I can always find two folks to help—four handles may not hold the dish, and twelve handles requires a football team to get it out of the oven.

Temperature Control

Most dishes are cooked at about 350 degrees, so except for a few dishes that require high temperatures, I *always* arrange the coals (charcoal briquettes) evenly around the outside edge of the oven, both on the lid and under the oven. I do this because it's simple and easy to remember, and because it never fails; the dynamics of cast iron insure that the heat is transferred evenly.

An important issue in Dutch oven cooking is temperature control, especially for novice cooks. For most meat and potato dishes, the cook does not need to be extra careful using the correct number of coals, but in baking breads and cakes it is important to use the correct amount of heat. Because heat rises, you need to force more heat from above to get an even inside temperature.

The number of coals you need depends on the size of your oven. Simply double the size of the oven. For example, 24 coals for a 12-inch. To get to 350 degrees, place ⅔ (16) of the coals on the lid around the edge and ⅓ (8) underneath, just under the edge. If you need more or less heat, just add or subtract two coals, one coal on top and one underneath, for each 25-degree increment.

When you think about it, most recipes you bake or roast in your home kitchen oven are cooked at 350 degrees, so the number of coals needed to heat 10-inch, 12-inch, and 14-inch ovens to 350 degrees is easy to calculate by simply doubling the oven size. Probably 95% of backyard cooking is done in one of these three oven sizes. If it's the middle of winter, that's okay: just fire up your kitchen oven to 50 degrees hotter than whatever temperature is called for, and when you add the Dutch oven, drop to the target temperature. Bake pies without the lid.

Remember, "Cast iron careth not from whence the heat cometh!"

Here are some common rules for the most common ovens.

10-inch oven: 21 coals total for 350 degrees
     7 coals underneath and 14 on the lid
     To add 50 degrees, just add 4 more coals, 2 underneath and 2 on the lid

12-inch oven: 24 coals total for 350 degrees
     8 coals underneath and 16 on the lid
     To add 50 degrees, just add 4 more coals, 2 underneath and 2 on the lid

14-inch oven: 28 coals total for 350 degrees
     9 coals underneath and 19 on the lid
     To add 50 degrees, just add 6 more coals, 3 underneath and 3 on the lid

Finally, after you have all of your equipment together, gather all of the ingredients and put them on your counter. I use a half-sheet pan and line everything up so I can see what I'm going to use. There is nothing worse for any cook than getting into the cupboard for your next ingredient and finding you are out of it. I have made many quick trips to the local supermarket in a panic, hoping I would get back in time to save the dish. The culinary term for avoiding this is *mise en place*, which just French for *prep every dish before you make it*.

One more thing. Read every recipe before you try it! This step will save you every time. (-:[>

Sleeping out in our backyard during the summer months was a rite of passage when I was a teenager. Friends would bring their sleeping bags and spread them out on our back lawn to spend the night in the great outdoors!

After spending the night not sleeping, we would arise to the sound of the rooster next door in the Stone's barn and spend much of the morning deciding what to do that day.

My dad was the family cook and he would often make breakfast for the mighty campers in a Dutch oven. Most meals were some kind of ham/bacon/sausage concoction that usually had cheese (read: Velveeta), and sometimes eggs, and maybe potatoes—or all of the above. Once in a while he would just cook bacon and eggs on the lid.

Chapter 1: Breakfast Dishes

Sausage and Hash Browns

12-inch oven

3 link sausages per person
1 package of hash brown potatoes
    (Or, if you want, shred 1 big russet potato per person and soak in water while
    cooking the sausage. Drain the potatoes and press between paper towels to get
    them as dry as you can just before cooking.)
2 Tbsp. butter

Fry the sausages in a 12-inch oven over 12 coals. Remove to a paper towel–covered plate; add the butter and potatoes to the pot.

Cook until slightly crispy. Return the sausages and serve with fry sauce on the side.

Fry Sauce

2 Tbsp. Miracle Whip
enough ketchup to turn the mix pink, one squirt at a time.
½ tsp. mustard powder

Mix all ingredients together.

Mountain Man Breakfast #1

This dish was my favorite dish when I started cooking in Dutch ovens. It is still a family favorite. The original recipe written by the late Val Cowley and Marie Cowley of Logan, Utah.

12-inch oven
8 coals underneath and 16 on the lid
350 degrees in your home oven

1 lb. bacon, diced to ½-inch pieces
1 stick butter, melted
1 medium yellow onion, diced small
½ loaf bread, any kind, cubed (the drier the better)
2 cups shredded cheese (your favorite)
10 eggs, lightly stirred
2 cups milk
2 Tbsp. mustard powder
½ tsp. salt

Fry the bacon in a 12-inch oven over 12 coals until barely crisp. Remove with a slotted spoon and drain on paper towels. Discard all but about 1 tablespoon of the grease. Add the butter and onion and cook until just soft.

Add the bread and cheese and toss until coated. Combine the eggs with the milk, mustard, and salt. Pour evenly over the bread/cheese. Evenly sprinkle the bacon over the top.

Cook with 8 coals underneath and 16 coals on top for 20–30 minutes, until the eggs set.

Serves 6–8

Breakfast Surprise

"The bacon will get the flavor started on the bottom and the moisture comes from the vegetables."
   – Gary Smith, Hurricane, Utah

The easiest way to assemble this dish is to preform the sausage balls and precut the vegetables.

12-inch oven
8 coals underneath and 16 on the lid
350 degrees in your home oven

1 lb. bacon, chilled well and diced to ½-inch while cold
3–4 large red potatoes, peeled (or not), diced to ½ inch
1½ lbs. Italian sausage
1 large white onion, sliced thin
1 green bell pepper, sliced
1 package Pillsbury® Grande rolls
pepper on each layer (fresh ground if you have a pepper mill)

Set the oven on 10 coals. It will slowly heat up. Slice the bacon into ½-inch pieces; spread evenly in Dutch oven bottom. If the bacon starts to sizzle before you get everything in the oven, pull the oven from the heat while you add the rest of the ingredients.

Spread the potatoes on the bacon.

Form the sausage into 1-inch meatballs with a #50 ice cream scoop and spread evenly on top of the potatoes. Add the onions and bell peppers. Evenly place the rolls on top.

Cook with the same 10 coals under and 14 on top until the coals are about dead, 50–60 minutes. Check at 45 minutes, and when the rolls start to brown, remove the oven from the coals and let the oven sit with the lid on for 15 minutes.

Optional: Grate about 4 ounces of any cheese and spread on the top at the end of cooking.

Serves 7

Mountain Man Breakfast Supreme

This is a "real man" quiche that we make when we have too many eggs. It doesn't require a crust, so it is fairly easy to prepare.

12-inch oven
8 coals underneath and 16 on the lid
350 degrees in your home oven

1 lb. bacon (dice while cold to ½-inch thick)
1 Tbsp. room temperature butter
1 yellow onion, sliced any way you want
1 green pepper, diced small
2–5 jalapeños, seeded and minced (start with 2 and work your way up until you have
    enough heat.)
15 eggs
8 oz. shredded Monterey Jack cheese
16 oz. small-curd cottage cheese
½ cup flour
1 tsp. baking powder
1 small jar pimentos, drained

Cook the bacon by putting it in a cold 12-inch oven. Evenly arrange 12 coals underneath and fry until just crisp. Remove with a slotted spoon and set aside on paper towels to drain.

Discard all but 1 tablespoon of the bacon grease and add the butter. When the butter gets hot, add the onion and peppers and sauté 5 minutes, stirring constantly.

While cooking the onions and peppers, whisk the eggs, cheeses, flour, and baking powder in a separate bowl until well blended. Stir in the pimentos and the bacon.

Gently pour over the pepper/onion mixture. Bake with 8 coals underneath and 16 on the lid around the edge for 50 minutes. Check with a table knife at 45 minutes. When the eggs are almost set, remove the coals. Leave in the oven for 10 minutes with the lid on and serve with a little hot sauce and shredded cheese of your choice.

Serves 6–10

Sausage and Eggs Mountain Man Breakfast

If it's January (when this recipe was written) and 10 degrees outside, just pop this into your preheated 400-degree home oven and drop to 350 when you put the pot in. It's a bit like a quiche with potatoes. We like this dish served with sour cream and salsa on the side.

12-inch oven
8 coals underneath and 16 on the lid
350 degrees in your home oven

½ lb. quality bacon, diced to ½-inch
1 (8-oz.) package Jimmy Dean or similar sausage patties
1 large onion, peeled and diced
1 bell pepper, chopped
4 russet potatoes, peeled (or not) and cubed
1 Tbsp. mustard powder
1 tsp. black pepper
1 tsp. salt
12 large eggs, lightly stirred
1 cup shredded cheese, your choice

Put the bacon in a cold 12-inch Dutch oven and place 12 coals underneath. Cook until crisp. Remove paper towels, drain all but 2 tablespoons bacon grease, and fry the sausage until just brown on both sides. Set aside with the bacon. Add onions and peppers to the oven and cook for 2 minutes. Add the potatoes and cook for 5 more minutes, stirring occasionally.

In a large mixing bowl, whisk the eggs with 1 tablespoon of water, mustard powder, pepper, and salt. Pour over the potato mix and stir in the bacon. Place the sausage patties on top.

Remove 4 coals from under the oven and put on the lid. Add 12 more to the lid and cook for 50 minutes.

When the eggs are set the way you want, remove the oven from the coals, sprinkle with your favorite grated cheese, and put the lid back on for 5 minutes until the cheese melts.

Serves 7–8

Real Man Dutch Oven Quiche

I like quiche in all of its forms, simply because the variations are endless. This one uses refrigerator rolls, making it easy to prepare.

12-inch oven
8 coals underneath and 16 on the lid
350 degrees in your home oven

1 lb. bacon, diced to ½-inch
1 cup (½ lb.) diced ham
1 (12-oz.) package breakfast link sausage cut into ½-inch pieces
1 large yellow onion, sliced or diced
1 red or green bell pepper, sliced or diced
1 jalapeño, seeded and minced (optional)
2 packages Pillsbury® Grande rolls
1 dozen eggs
½ tsp. salt
½ tsp. black pepper
1 cup of your favorite shredded cheese

Place 12 coals under a 12-inch oven. Add the bacon to the cold oven and fry until crisp. Remove with a slotted spoon and set aside on a paper towel–covered plate to drain. Drain most of the bacon grease, add the sausage pieces, and cook until done. Add the ham, onions, and peppers and cook until the onions are soft, about 5 minutes. Add this to the bacon and sausage on the paper towels with a slotted spoon. Remove the oven from the coals, drain the remaining grease, and let it cool off a bit. When you can handle the oven with your bare hands, place seven of the rolls snugly in the bottom of the oven. Press out evenly. Cut in half 6 rolls in the second can of Grandes and press along the sides of the oven.

In a large bowl, whisk eggs with the salt and pepper and add the meat, onions, and peppers.

Pour into the oven. Place the oven back on 8 coals underneath and add 16 on the lid. Cook for about 45 minutes. Check at about 35 minutes to see if the rolls are browning. As soon as they are light brown, sprinkle the cheese over the top and replace the lid for 5 minutes while the cheese melts. Remove the oven from the coals, wait 5 more minutes with the lid off, and serve.

Serves 10–12

Scotch Eggs

Scots farmers in the Middle Ages took these to work in the fields so they wouldn't have to return home for lunch, saving time. You can make these the night before for work or school lunches. We like to make them for lunch on all-day ATV rides when we don't get back until evening.

12-inch oven
8 coals underneath and 16 on the lid
350 degrees in your home oven

8 hard-boiled eggs, peeled and cooled
2 lbs. bulk breakfast sausage
1 cup flour
2 eggs with 1 Tbsp. water
1 cup panko crumbs
1 tsp. kosher salt
1 tsp. ground black pepper

Cut the sausage into 8 equal ¼-lb. pieces and form each loosely into a ball. After you form them, put on a plate and refrigerate for 1 hour. Take one sausage ball out of the refrigerator and make a big indentation in the ball with your thumb. Gently work it into a bowl-shape, keeping the sausage thickness as even as you can all the way around. Roll a hard-boiled egg in the flour and place into the sausage bowl, gently forming it completely around the egg.

Put back into the refrigerator and do the rest of the eggs one at a time. Leave them in the refrigerator for 30 minutes.

Combine the other two eggs and water in a bowl. Put the panko crumbs in a small bowl. Stir in the salt and pepper. Dip a sausage-wrapped egg in the egg wash and then roll it around in the bread crumbs until they are heavily covered. Repeat for all of the eggs. Put 12 coals under a 12-inch oven. Add the scotch eggs and fry, turning them until they are brown on all sides. Take 4 of the coals from under the oven, put them on the lid, add 12 more coals to the lid, and cook for 30 minutes.

Serve with fry sauce (page 118) or your favorite condiment.

Serves 4

Basic Yeast Bread

Many Dutch oven cooks are intimidated by bread making. Don't let that slow you down. Baking bread is as easy as starting with a 5:3 ratio, by weight. Flour weighs about 5 ounces per cup and water is 8 ounces per cup. For example, 4 cups (20 oz.) flour and 1½ cups (12 oz.) liquid is a basic starter dough. The only other things it needs are yeast and a bit of salt. That is all you need to make basic yeast bread.

One thing worth remembering is that yeast dough is hard to overwork when kneading by hand. It is very forgiving. Your arms will seize up before you can ruin the dough. Just make sure the loaf is a bit rubbery and smooth. The things you can do with raised bread dough are limitless.

Quick Bread Ratios

Most quick breads, like muffins and banana bread, use this basic ratio by weight: 2 parts flour, 2 parts liquid, 1 part egg, and 1 part fat. You don't need a fancy scale. A cup of flour weighs about 5 ounces, an egg weighs 2 ounces, and sugar and fat weigh what they say. Just remember the egg is constant because you can't cut it, so you have to adjust the other ingredients to the egg.

One last note. When any bread is done, leave it in the oven with the lid off for 10 minutes and then on a rack to cool for 30 minutes more.

Chapter 2: Breads

Basic No-Knead Bread

We make this easy, great-tasting bread several times a week. One of the side benefits is that the rising time is so long that the finished bread has a slight sourdough taste. The main idea here is that you use equal amounts (by weight) of flour and water. You use very little yeast because of the long fermentation time. Flour weighs about 5.5 oz. per cup and water weighs 8 oz. per cup. The rest is easy!

10-inch oven
12 coals underneath and 20 on the lid
450 degrees in your kitchen oven

3 cups bread flour
¼ tsp. instant yeast
1 tsp. salt
2 cups water

Combine the dry ingredients in a large mixing bowl. Add the water and mix well. It will be very loose. Cover the bowl with plastic and let sit 8–12 hours. I do this in the morning or the night before.

When you're ready to bake, transfer from the bowl to a big nonstick pan and put a lid on it.

Meanwhile, preheat your 10-inch Dutch oven for 20 minutes with 12 coals underneath and 20 coals on the lid. If you're using your home oven, preheat to 450 with the Dutch oven on the center rack.

By the time the Dutch oven is hot enough (heated either way), the dough will be ready to transfer to the pot.

If you bake this in your kitchen oven, carefully (!) take the very hot Dutch oven out of the oven, transfer the dough from the nonstick pan to the Dutch oven, and smooth it a bit with a spatula. Put the lid on and cook for 30 minutes, then check its temperature with a meat thermometer. 190–200 degrees is what you want.

You can add almost anything to this dough, from savory to sweet!

Serves 8–10

Bread Sticks

Any time I make pizza, I make these with whatever dough I have left over. You can top them with anything, from jam to cheeses. Or . . . you can make a whole batch at once.

12-inch oven
10 underneath and 20 coals on the lid
425 degrees in your home oven

1 cup warm water
2 Tbsp. vegetable oil
3–4 cups bread flour
1 package instant yeast
1 Tbsp. sugar
1 tsp. salt

To prepare the dough, mix the water and oil in a large mixing bowl.

In another bowl, combine 3 cups flour with yeast, sugar, and salt. Add 1 cup of this mix to the water and stir vigorously for at least 30 seconds. Slowly add more flour mixture one cup at a time until it starts to pull away from the sides of the bowl.

Knead it on a lightly floured board for 5 minutes. When it gets a bit rubbery, cover and let sit for 30 minutes to rise and hydrate.

Roll out to a rectangle and place on a pizza pan or cookie sheet. Cut into strips with the tip of a sharp knife or pizza cutter, twist or bend them any way you want, and let rise one more time for 30 minutes.

Bake in a 12-inch oven at 425 degrees with 10 coals underneath and 20 on the lid for 15 minutes.

Brush with butter and top with kosher salt, Parmesan cheese, Italian seasoning, or any combination thereof. For a sweet touch, try powdered sugar, honey, or any jam or jelly.

Serves 5–6

Cheese Onion Rolls

This recipe was my first real success with the Dutch oven, when I realized that the oven was round and most rolls did not fit into it very well.

12-inch oven
8 coals underneath and 16 on the lid
350 degrees in your home oven

1 cup warm water
¼ cup sugar
1 Tbsp. vegetable oil
1 tsp. salt
2 eggs, divided
1 package instant yeast
3–4 cups flour
1 medium red onion, chopped fine
4 oz. extra-sharp cheddar cheese, shredded
1 green or red bell pepper, sliced or diced (optional)
various other fillings; bacon, sausage, etc (optional)
2 Tbsp. sesame seeds (optional)
egg wash (stir together 1 egg and 1 Tbsp. water, optional glue for the sesame seeds)
nonstick cooking spray

Mix water, sugar, oil, salt, 1 egg, and yeast. Add 2 cups of flour until incorporated and then stir vigorously for about 30 seconds. Add up to 2 more cups of flour ½ cup at a time until you have soft dough that pulls away from the sides of the bowl. Knead on a board with a little flour until the dough is well formed and elastic, 4–5 minutes. Shape into a ball and roll around in an oiled bowl. Cover and let rise until almost double.

While the dough is rising, chop the onions and shred the cheese.

Set aside to dry out a bit.

When the dough has risen once, sprinkle a little flour on the board and spread dough out to about a 12- to 15-inch-wide rectangle. I do this with my hands. Spray lightly with nonstick cooking spray and spread with onion and cheese mix. Roll up from the long side, jelly roll–style.

Cut into triangles.

Spray a 12-inch oven with nonstick cooking spray. Arrange the rolls in a circle, just touching.

Sprinkle some dry parsley over them. If you want sesame seeds, brush with egg wash before the second rise and sprinkle with the seeds. Let rise again until almost double. Bake at 350 degrees for about 45 minutes. Use 8 coals on the bottom and 16 on the lid. Lift the pot and rotate it, and then the lid, every ten minutes for more even baking.

After 30 minutes, check the rolls for browning. When they begin to brown, pull the bottom coals. When they are golden brown, pull the rest of the coals from the top. Leave them in the oven with the lid off for about 10 minutes after the heat is removed. Turn out and move to a rack to cool.

Makes 12 rolls. ENJOY!

Note: You can change the types of cheese and onion. For a softer crust, you can brush the rolls with butter while they are still hot.

Really Easy White Rolls

This is Gary Smith's (Hurricane, Utah) famous baking invention. The first time I tried these was in our backyard at an Easter dinner, complete with an Easter egg hunt for the grandkids. This is one recipe that does better if you leave the lid off when you bake it in your home oven.

12-inch oven
10 underneath and 18 coals on the lid
400 degrees in your home oven

6 cans refrigerated rolls
butter
kosher salt

Open each can and place in the oven on end.

Pour the heat to it . . . 10 coals underneath and 18 coals on the lid.

Check them at 20 minutes and pull the coals when they start to brown. When they are golden brown, brush the rolls with butter and sprinkle with kosher salt.

Serve from the pot. Once you get the first one out, it's easy.

Serves 15+

Easy Banana Bread

Sometimes we want a light dessert for breakfast or a midday snack. This banana bread fits the bill! Covered, it will keep for several days.

12-inch oven
8 underneath and 16 coals on the lid
350 degrees in your home oven

5–6 overripe bananas, mashed
2 cups sugar
4 eggs
1 cup melted butter
1 cup milk
2 tsp. vanilla
4 cups flour
1 tsp. salt
3 Tbsp. baking powder
1 tsp. baking soda
1 cup chopped nuts (optional)

Beat the bananas, sugar and eggs together. Add the butter; stir in milk and vanilla.

In a large bowl, whisk the dry ingredients together.

Pour in the wet ingredients all at once and mix just until just wet. Fold in the nuts if you have them.

Spray a 12-inch oven with nonstick cooking spray. Add a parchment ring and spray that too.

Carefully pour in the batter.

Bake about 1 hour with 6 coals under just under the edge and 16 coals on the lid around the edge. Spin the lid and the oven a few times while it's baking.

When the trusty old toothpick tests dry, it's done (or you can use a table knife or even a skewer).

Let it sit in the oven for a few minutes and turn out onto the lid. Set the lid on a trivet.

Peel off the parchment paper and serve.

Try some banana-flavored ice cream on the side.

Easy White Rolls

These rolls are a quick way to serve raised bread with dinner. Use a 12-inch regular oven, or if you only have a deep one, add 2 more coals to the lid. Remember to save ¼ cup melted butter for dipping the dough when you form the rolls.

12-inch oven
8 underneath and 16 coals on the lid
350 degrees in your home oven

1 cup warm water
¼ cup honey
¾ cup melted butter, divided
1 tsp. salt
2 large eggs, lightly beaten
2 packages instant yeast
3–4 cups flour, divided

In a large bowl, combine the water, honey, and yeast. Whisk in ½ cup melted butter, salt, and eggs. Add 1 cup of flour to the wet ingredients and mix thoroughly for about 30 seconds. Switch to a wooden spoon and slowly add more flour 1 cup at a time until the dough pulls away from the sides of the bowl.

Knead for about a minute on a lightly floured board, form into a ball, cover with plastic wrap, and let it rest for 10 minutes while you prepare another dinner dish.

Form into 2½ inch balls with a #10 ice cream scoop, dip into remaining melted butter, and place each ball in a sprayed 12-inch oven so that they're just touching. Allow to rise approximately 30 minutes, or until double in size.

Bake for about 25 minutes with 8 coals underneath and 16 on the lid, until the rolls are golden brown.

Flip out onto the oven lid to cool. Brush the tops with melted butter while still hot and sprinkle with a little kosher salt. Serve warm if time permits.

Serves differently sized rolls for 12

Frozen Dough Rolls

This is the easy way to bake rolls if you are not in a hurry. It may seem to take forever for them to rise, but rise they will.

12-inch oven
8 coals underneath and 16 on the lid
350 degrees in your home oven

1 package frozen Texas Rolls dough balls, use 11 balls
egg wash, 1 egg mixed with 1 Tbsp. water
sesame seeds
½ stick butter, melted

Place frozen dough balls in a sprayed 12-inch oven and set somewhere warm for a few hours.

When they have risen fully, carefully brush egg wash and sprinkle sesame seeds over the rolls.

Bake with 8 coals underneath and 16 on the lid for 30 minutes. When they are golden brown, brush with butter and serve.

Ice Cream Bread

This one comes from my cousin Mary in Colorado. She and her husband Randy have a bed and break-fast near Estes Park. It's very easy to make, as there are only six ingredients. You can use self-rising flour instead of the flour and baking soda. We like ice cream with nuts of some kind.

10-inch oven
7 coals underneath and 14 on the lid
350 degrees in your home oven

3 cups flour
2 Tbsp. baking powder
2 tsp. salt
¼ cup sugar
1 quart ice cream, softened (choose your favorite flavor and refrigerate overnight)
¾ cup milk

Mix the dry ingredients together. Add the ice cream and milk and mix until just combined.

Spray a 10-inch oven with Pam, put a parchment paper ring in the bottom, and spray that too.

Get a big serving spoon and spread the batter evenly in a 10-inch oven. It will be quite thick.

Bake with 14–15 coals on top and 7–8 coals under for about 45 minutes.

Check it with a big toothpick or a knife.

When it's done, let it cool in the pot with the lid off for ten minutes.

Put the lid back on and flip it over onto the lid.

Let it cool completely, cut it any way you want, and serve with some ice cream or jam.

Serves 8

Mormon Muffin Apple Cake

This is from the famous Mormon Muffin recipe at the Greenery restaurant in Ogden, Utah. Make the batter and refrigerate the night before to give it time to absorb the liquid.

12-inch oven
8 underneath and 16 coals on the lid
350 degrees in your home oven

1 Tbsp. baking soda
1 cup boiling water
½ cup (1 stick) butter, room temperature
1 cup sugar
2 eggs
2 cups buttermilk
½ tsp. vanilla
2½ cups flour
½ tsp. salt
2 Granny Smith apples, peeled and diced small
2 cups All-Bran cereal
1 cup 40% Bran Flakes cereal
½ cup chopped walnuts (optional)

Add baking soda to boiling water and set aside. In a large bowl, whip butter and sugar together until light and fluffy. Add the eggs, one at a time, thoroughly mixing after each addition. Stir in the buttermilk, vanilla, flour, and salt. Add the baking soda and water mixture very slowly. Gently fold in the apples, walnuts, and cereals into the batter. Cover and refrigerate overnight to allow all of the liquid to absorb.

Spray a 12-inch oven with nonstick cooking spray and add a parchment paper ring and an empty soup can; spray the ring and add the batter with a big spoon (the batter will be very thick). Cover and bake, using 8 coals underneath the oven and 16 coals on the lid, for 40 minutes. Every 15 minutes, gently turn the oven about a quarter-turn over the coals, and then turn the lid the opposite direction to prevent hot spots. Near the end of baking time, poke the cake with a table knife to test for doneness. If it's still a bit wet, just put the lid back on for 10 minutes. When done, leave cake in the oven with the lid off for a few minutes and then turn out onto the lid or a rack to cool. Drizzle the finished cake with one of the fruit sauces (chapter 7) or your sauce of choice.

Cut this up in 8 or 16 pieces

Oatmeal Raisin Pecan Cookie

This is simply the recipe from the Quaker Oats box, modified so you can bake it in a Dutch oven. It makes one (really) big cookie. You can add any dried fruit and nuts you like.

12-inch oven
8 coals underneath and 16 coals on the lid
350 degrees in your home oven

¾ cup butter (1½ sticks), room temperature
1 cup brown sugar
½ cup sugar
2 Tbsp. corn oil
2 eggs
1 tsp. vanilla
2 cups all-purpose flour
1 tsp. baking soda
1 tsp. cinnamon
½ tsp. salt
3 cups uncooked oatmeal, any style
1 cup raisins (optional)
1 cup pecans (optional)

In a large mixing bowl, cream the butter and sugars. Add the oil and mix well.

Add the eggs one at a time until each is incorporated.

In a separate bowl combine flour, baking soda, cinnamon, and salt.

Add this to the mix and stir until smooth, then fold in oats, raisins and pecans.

Put a parchment paper ring in a 12-inch oven. Spoon mix into the oven.

Bake 8 coals underneath with 16 coals on the lid for 15–20 minutes.

Check at 15 minutes for golden brown. Leave up to 20 minutes. When it is ready, pull all of the coals and let it sit with the lid on for 5 minutes. Run a kitchen knife around the inside edge of the oven, tip the oven to remove, and cool on a wire rack.

Cut it into 8–16 pieces and serve with cold milk.

Orange Caramel Bubble Crown

We won a cook-off hands down where this was the bread entry. You need a #50 ice cream scoop.

12-inch oven
8 coals underneath and 16 on the lid
350 degrees in your home oven

2 packages instant yeast
4–6 cups flour, divided
1½ cups warm water
¼ cup sugar
1 teaspoon salt
2 tablespoons vegetable oil
2 eggs, lightly beaten
8-oz. bag individually wrapped caramel candy pieces
½ cup whipping cream
juice and zest from 1 orange
2 small boxes butterscotch cooked pudding mix, not instant
½ cup (1 stick) butter, melted
8 oz. pecan pieces, chopped

In a large bowl, mix yeast with 2 cups flour. Combine water, sugar, salt, oil, and eggs in a small bowl and then add 2 cups flour. Stir vigorously for 30 seconds. Add more flour, 1 cup at a time, until you have a soft dough. Knead on a floured board until the dough is well formed and a bit elastic. Place in a large oiled bowl; cover with plastic wrap and a towel. Let rise until almost double in size. While the dough is rising, unwrap and slowly melt caramels in a small saucepan with the cream, orange juice, and zest. Empty the pudding mix packets into a small bowl. Spray the inside of Dutch oven with nonstick cooking spray.

Place an empty small fruit can in the middle of the oven. Punch down dough and make 1-inch balls about the size of a ping pong ball; a #50 ice cream scoop works well. Dip each ball in melted butter and roll in the dry pudding mix.

Arrange about half of the dough balls around the can. Evenly sprinkle the pecans and pour the caramel sauce over this layer. Place the rest of the dough balls as the second layer.

Let rise again until double in size, 30–40 minutes. Cover and bake, using 8 coals underneath and 16 coals on the lid, for 45 minutes. Every 15 minutes, gently turn the oven about a quarter-turn over the coals, and then turn the lid the opposite direction to prevent hot spots.

Remove the bottom coals after 30 minutes.

When the bread turns a golden brown on top, remove all of the coals. Let the oven sit with the lid on for about 5 minutes and then invert onto the lid or a serving platter.

Serves 8–15

Vickie's Three-Cheese Sourdough Bread

My wife, Vickie, loves sourdough bread and suggested once that I add some cheese, so here it is. This sourdough bread recipe works great in a Dutch oven. The addition of instant yeast speeds up the process so you don't wait several hours for the dough to rise.

12-inch oven
8 coals underneath and 18 on the lid
350 degrees in your home oven

2 Tbsp. sugar
1 cup warm water
1 cup sourdough starter (I use the one by Carl Griffith's family, which has been around
      since 1847—visit www.carlsfriends.net to get some)
½ tsp. dried oregano
1½ tsp. salt
¼ cup ricotta cheese
1 Tbsp. vegetable oil
½ cup grated sharp cheddar cheese
½ cup freshly grated Parmesan cheese
½ cup chopped green onion
1 package instant yeast
4–5 cups unbleached bread flour
egg wash, 1 egg and 1 tsp. water
sesame seeds (optional)

In a large bowl, combine water and sugar. Stir in the starter. In a small bowl, mix together the oregano, salt, ricotta cheese, oil, cheddar cheese, Parmesan cheese, and green onion. Stir into the sourdough mixture. Add 1 cup flour and yeast and stir vigorously for at least 30 seconds. Add more flour, 1 cup at a time, until dough pulls away from the sides of the bowl.

Knead the dough on a hard flat surface with a little flour until it forms a smooth ball and is a bit elastic. Spray a large bowl with nonstick cooking spray and add the dough ball, rolling around until coated with oil. Cover, set aside in a warm place, and let it rise until almost double in size.

Form the dough into a ball, place in Dutch oven, and brush with egg wash. Sprinkle with sesame seeds, if using. Let it rise until almost double again, about 30 minutes or more.

When the dough is ready, slash the top several times with a wet razor blade or a small serrated knife. Cover and bake, using 8 coals underneath the oven and 18 coals on top, for about 30–40 minutes. Every 15 minutes, gently turn the oven about a quarter-turn over the coals and then turn the lid the opposite direction to prevent hot spots.

The bread is done when you flick it with your finger and it sounds hollow, or a probe thermometer reads 190 degrees. Let it sit in the hot oven with the lid off for a few minutes and then turn out onto a wire rack to cool. Let it cool completely before slicing.

Serves 10–12

Easiest Stuffed Cornbread

We like cornbread, cheese, and sausage, so this dish is perfect as a side dish at family gatherings. You can substitute just about any type of ground meat and cheese.

12-inch oven
10 underneath and 18 coals on the lid
400 in your home oven

1 lb. Italian sausage
1 medium onion, diced small
1 medium bell pepper, chopped small
salt and pepper
3 packages cornbread muffin mix
12 slices cheddar cheese singles
3 jalapeños, chopped fine (optional)
Sriracha sauce (optional)

Brown meat with onion and bell pepper in skillet. Add salt and pepper to taste. Drain and set aside. Squirt as much optional Sriracha over the meat mix as you want. Prepare the muffin mixes as directed in large mixing bowl.

Add a parchment ring (page XI) to a 12-inch oven and pour in half of cornbread batter.

Place 6 slices of cheese over batter. Spread meat mixture over cheese evenly.

Add optional jalapeños, if desired. Top with remaining slices of cheese. Pour the rest of the batter on top.

If you are using your kitchen oven for this, preheat to 425 and drop to 400 when you add the pot. Check at 20 minutes with a table knife and add 5 more minutes with the lid off if not done.

Bake for 20 to 25 minutes with 10 coals underneath and 18 on the lid until brown on top. Let cool for about 10 minutes and serve.

Serves 8

We all love the simple fare of a hearty soup in midwinter paired with a grilled cheese sandwich while we watch our favorite weekday prime time drama or movie. The greatest advantage of cooking in a Dutch oven is the enhanced flavor. With the tight-fitting lid in place while simmering, the essential oils stay in the food instead of floating around the house. Many of these recipes use ingredients likely already in your cupboard and refrigerator, and most let you substitute some ingredients to modify the flavors to your taste. As a general rule, soups and chilis don't have a strict timeline for preparation, so you are free to concentrate on other parts of the meal, like which cheese to use for the accompanying sandwiches. I'm a dipper, so any sandwich is always dipped in whatever soup or chili is in the bowl.

Chapter 3: Soups and Chilies

Easiest Beef Chili

I love chili, and the easier the better. Sometimes I cook it without beans.

2 lbs. 85% hamburger
salt and pepper
1 large sweet onion, half chopped, half sliced, divided
1 Tbsp. minced garlic (I get mine from a jar)
2 (1-oz.) packages chili mix
1 Tbsp. paprika
1 tsp. dried oregano
1 (14-oz.) can diced tomatoes
3 (15-oz.) cans dark kidney beans

Heat a 12-inch Dutch oven over 12 coals. Add the beef and cook until browned, 5 minutes.

Season with salt and pepper. Add the chopped part of the onion. Cook, stirring frequently, until onions wilt a bit, 5 minutes. Add the rest of the ingredients and the sliced part of the onion. Remove 4 coals from under the oven, add 16 coals to the lid, and cook until the coals are about dead, 45 minutes, stirring occasionally.

You can also do this on your kitchen stove or your propane camp stove.

Serves 6–10

Bell Pepper Dutch Oven Chili

This is the chili we like the most. It started as a competition recipe and morphed into this (fairly) simple dish.

12-inch Dutch oven—heat with charcoal or on any stove
12 coals on top and 12 underneath

2 lbs. lean ground chuck
6 Tbsp. chili powder, divided
1 Tbsp. cumin
½ cup butter (one stick), divided
1 large red (or white, or yellow) onion, thinly sliced
1 each red, green and yellow (or any combination) bell peppers, seeded and thinly sliced
2 Tbsp. minced garlic, divided (I buy mine in a jar)
2 (14.5-oz.) cans diced tomatoes
1 Tbsp. vinegar
salt and pepper

In a large bowl, mix the beef with 4 tablespoons (¼ cup) of the chili powder and a pinch of salt. Set aside. In a large frying pan, heat ½ stick butter over medium heat until it just starts to bubble a bit. Add the onions and green peppers. Sauté until the onions are translucent, 5 minutes. Stir in one tablespoon garlic and cook for one more minute.

Add the other half-stick butter to a 12-inch oven over 12 coals. Wait for the butter to heat up and add the beef. Cook, stirring continuously, until it is mostly browned. Add enough water to cover the meat. Cover and cook with the same coals for 30 minutes. Add 1 can tomatoes, red bell pepper slices, the other tablespoon of the garlic, and the cumin.

When this mix heats enough to start boiling, stir in the other can tomatoes, the rest of the chili powder, the rest of the garlic, the vinegar, and the sautéed garlic/onions. Cook until the coals are dead, 30 minutes, or simmer on the stove for 30 minutes.

Season and serve. Try a dollop of sour cream.

Side note: If your meat is a bit fatty and there is too much floating grease, spoon most of it out, mix 2 tablespoons flour with ¼ cup water, and stir into the chili. Simmer 15 minutes to cook the flour. If you want a raw onion–mouth feel, dice another ½ onion and add near the end of cooking.

Serves 12 (or 6 chili-heads)

Cream of Chicken Soup

We do several dishes with a store-bought rotisserie chicken. Just bone it and go. You can cook this wonderful, satisfying soup with charcoal or on your kitchen stove! This recipe is for the kitchen stove because it is winter here as I write this. If you have a glass-top stove be careful not to drop your pot on it. Disaster!

10-inch oven
If you cook this in the backyard, put 10 coals underneath.

1 stick butter, sliced into 8 pieces, divided
1 Tbsp. extra virgin olive oil
1 large onion, diced
1 carrot, peeled and sliced
2 ribs celery, diced
2 qts. water
1 cup flour
2 Tbsp. chicken bouillon
½ pound melty cheese (Velveeta), sliced
1 rotisserie chicken, boned

Melt 4 tablespoons butter and olive oil in a 10-inch oven until it starts to bubble. Add the onion, carrots, and celery and stir for 5 minutes until you can smell the aroma of the mirepoix.

In a large bowl, mix the flour and water and add to the vegetables. Heat to simmering and add the bouillon and Velveeta.

When the cheese melts, stir in the remaining butter and chicken. Continue to stir for about 15 minutes.

Serve with crackers or chips.

Serves 10–12

Easiest Kicked-Up Chicken Soup

This is just packaged soup with mirepoix and chicken added. It can be prepared in about as much time as it takes to bone the chicken.

10 coals underneath (or on your camp stove outside or your stovetop inside)

Mirepoix
1 Tbsp. butter with 1 tsp. olive oil
2 ribs celery, chopped
1 small onion, diced
1 carrot, chopped small

Soup
2 qts. water
1 rotisserie chicken, separate the meat from the bones
2 packages Lipton noodle soup
salt
pepper

Start the butter and oil in a 10-inch oven over 10 coals; add the veggies, season with salt and pepper, and sauté for 5 minutes. Add the water and bring to a simmer. Add the packages of noodle soup. Add the chicken, simmer for 5 minutes, and serve.

Serves 8–10

Smoked Turkey Soup

We usually have a smoked turkey as part of the Thanksgiving Day festivities. Leftover turkey is never as tasty as the original because it always dries out. This recipe takes care of the leftover turkey. Serve as a Black Friday dinner with sandwiches and freeze the rest in zip-lock bags.

2 lbs. potatoes, peeled and diced
1 cup baby carrots
3 ribs celery, diced
1 medium onion, sliced
4 cups reduced-sodium chicken broth
½ tsp. oregano
½ tsp. dried thyme leaves
4 cups (leftover) smoked turkey, roughly diced to ½ inch

Add all ingredients except the turkey to a 12-inch Dutch oven. Cook with 12 coals on the lid and 12 underneath for 30 minutes. Season with salt and pepper, add the turkey, and cook with the lid off for 10 more minutes.

Serves 12

Split Pea Soup

This was my favorite soup as a young boy. When I was 8 or 9, Grandma showed me how to boil the peas, and since then I've added everything under the sun at one time or another. As always, cooking in a Dutch oven traps the flavors in the food.

12-inch oven
12 coals underneath and 8 on the lid
Medium heat on your kitchen stove

2 cups reduced-sodium chicken broth
1 lb. dried split peas
2 cups diced ham
3 stalks celery, sliced thin
2 bell peppers, any color, diced
1 large onion, half sliced and half diced
1 bunch green onions, chopped
1 Tbsp. minced garlic (I get mine from a bottle)
½ tsp. thyme leaves
½ tsp. dried sage leaves

Rinse the peas first. Then, add all of the ingredients and enough water to cover by 1 inch. Stir and put the lid on. Place 12 coals underneath and 8 on the lid and cook, stirring occasionally, until the coals are about dead, 50–60 minutes. If you want a creamier soup, put 2 cups into a blender and purée until smooth. Return to the pot and simmer with 10 coals underneath with the lid off until the released starch naturally thickens the soup, 10–15 minutes.

Serve with any bread or cracker.

Tuscany Soup

Tuscany is a region in central Italy. A good friend showed me this soup during a string of blizzards that killed the power. The easiest way to cook this dish is on a (Camp Chef) propane stove. If you don't have propane, you can always use coals.

12-inch Dutch oven
Start with about 10 coals underneath and adjust if it gets too hot

2 lbs. Italian sausages, sliced to 1 inch (you can remove the casings before you slice)
1 (12-oz.) package bacon, cut into 1-inch pieces
4–5 russet potatoes, diced or sliced thin
1 large onion, sliced thin
1 (49-oz.) can low-sodium chicken broth (you'll need about 1½ quarts)
8 oz. sliced mushrooms
2 Tbsp. minced garlic (I get mine from a jar)
2 cups kale or Swiss chard, chopped
1 pint heavy whipping cream
¼ cup flour

Brown sausage for 5 minutes in a 12-inch oven over 10 coals. Remove and set aside to drain.

Fry bacon just to the crisp stage. Remove with a slotted spoon and set aside with the sausage to drain. Drain ½ of the bacon grease from the oven and cook the potatoes for 5 minutes, adding more bacon grease if needed.

Add all of the ingredients, except the chard/kale, cream, and flour to the oven and add just enough water to cover everything.

Simmer for 30 minutes until the potatoes are soft.

Meanwhile, in a small bowl mix the flour with the cream and stir until combined. When the potatoes are done, stir into the soup and add the chard/kale. Simmer for 20 minutes or until the soup begins to thicken.

Season with salt and pepper. If you have some white truffle oil, add ½ teaspoon near the end of cooking.

Serve immediately with crackers. (I like Ritz.)

Vegetable Beef Soup

This is a quick and easy classic soup. Just brown the beef and throw everything in the pot. You can kick it up by adding small amounts of herbs and spices. The easiest way is to cut everything and line it all up on the counter so you can see what you have.

12-inch oven
12 coals underneath or on any stove

1–2 lbs. lean chuck, cubed to 1 inch or so
2 Tbsp. vegetable oil
1 Tbsp. butter
1 onion, sliced or diced
1 carrot, peeled and sliced
4 ribs celery, diced to your preference
1 bell pepper, chopped
2 bunches green onions, chopped
8 oz. sliced mushrooms
2 russet potatoes, diced to ½ inch
1 (14-oz.) can diced tomatoes
¼ tsp. oregano/basil (optional)
⅛ tsp. thyme (optional)
32 oz. beef broth, plus enough water to cover everything by 1 inch
2 bay leaves
1 cup barley, pearl or flakes (optional)
beef bouillon (optional)

Place 12 coals underneath the oven and heat up the oil. Season the meat with salt and black pepper and brown for 1 minute, stirring twice. Add everything else, cover, and cook until the coals are about dead, maybe 60 minutes.

You can add a small amount of beef bouillon at the end to add some flavor. Remove the bay leaves and serve.

Serves 12

The recipes in this section are listed by main meat ingredient—beef, pork, chicken, etc.—so you can decide which you want. There are recipes here for the novice, intermediate, and advanced cooks. There is a little bit of everything, from simple meatloaf dishes to bacon lasagna that will bring tears to the bacon lover. You will be the favorite cook of your family and friends.

Sound advice: First, always read the entire recipe, top to bottom, before you start mixing anything; this will save you loads of time.

Second, gather all of the ingredients and equipment and place them on your counter before you start. If you don't, you will invariably forget something and waste time fetching it.

Third, always try to have the ingredients at room temperature. You don't want to be waiting around for the butter to warm up because you just took it out of the refrigerator.

Chapter 4: Main Dishes

Baked Ziti

This is the perfect dish for weekday potluck dinners. It's easy to prepare and is always a hit with the crowd. Read the recipe first and assemble the ingredients on the counter before you start. This is essentially a layered pasta dish similar to lasagna but quicker. It's a hundred times easier if you read the recipe first . . . every word!

12-inch oven
8 coals underneath and 16 on the lid
350 degrees in your home oven

1 lb. small penne or elbow macaroni (ziti pasta can be hard to find)
2 Tbsp. olive oil
1 large sweet onion, diced
½ small red onion, diced
1 stalk celery, sliced thin on the bias
1 lb. 85% ground chuck
1 lb. ground Italian sausage
1 green bell pepper, chopped
1 Tbsp. minced garlic (I get mine from a bottle)
1 (28-oz.) can Italian style diced tomatoes
1 (10-oz.) can diced tomatoes and green chiles
1 (15-oz.) can whole tomatoes
1 (14.5-oz.) can tomato sauce
1 tub (15-oz.) Ricotta cheese
2 lb. bag (4 cups) grated mozzarella cheese
½ cup Parmesan cheese
1 egg
¼ tsp. kosher salt
⅛ tsp. fresh ground pepper

Add the pasta to lightly salted boiling water and cook for 7–8 minutes to al dente.

Drain in a colander and rinse in cold water to stop the cooking. Set aside.

Heat oil in a 12-inch oven over 12 coals. Add onions and celery and sauté for 2 minutes, stirring continuously. Add ground beef, sausage, green pepper, and garlic and cook until meat is browned.

Drain and return to oven. Add diced tomatoes, whole tomatoes, tomatoes and green chiles, and tomato sauce. Cook for 30 minutes, stirring occasionally. Pour into large bowl and let it sit for 10 minutes to cool down and then spread 1 cup in the bottom of the oven.

While the sauce is cooling, mix the ricotta cheese in a large mixing bowl with 2 cups of the grated Mozzarella, Parmesan, egg, salt, and pepper until just combined.

Pour the pasta into the bowl with the cheese mixture and stir. Add three cups cooled meat sauce and fold in until combined. Add half of this pasta mixture to the Dutch oven.

Spoon half of the remaining sauce over the pasta and sprinkle with half the remaining mozzarella cheese. Repeat with the remaining pasta and the remaining sauce and top it with the remaining mozzarella.

Bake for 30 minutes with 8 coals underneath and 18 on the lid.

Pull the coals and let it rest for 10 minutes with the lid off.

Serve with French bread or sourdough bread.

Serves 10–12

Deep-Dish Mexican Pizza

I saw this somewhere on the internet and decided I could make it in a Dutch oven. After two tries, this is what came out of the modified recipe. We serve it with sour cream and our favorite salsa.

12-inch oven
8 coals underneath and 18 on the lid
375 degrees in your home oven.

1½ lb. lean ground chuck
1 green bell pepper, chopped
1 small yellow onion, diced small
½ cup water
2 (1-oz.) packages taco seasoning mix
4 oz. shredded cheddar cheese
2 (8-oz.) cans Pillsbury® refrigerated crescent dinner rolls

Garnish
1 cup shredded lettuce
½ cup chopped tomato
¼ cup sliced ripe olives
sour cream

Combine ground chuck, bell pepper, onion, water, and taco seasoning. Cook until the meat is browned nicely and the water is evaporated. Remove from heat and stir in cheese. Set aside.

Arrange a set of parchment paper lifts (page XII) in a sprayed 12-inch oven and spray them too.

Unroll both cans of dough and separate into 16 triangles. Arrange triangles in the oven, overlapping into wreath shape. Lightly press the overlapping middle to flatten. Spoon cooked ground chuck mix in a 3-inch circle in the oven, leaving a 4-inch hole. Pull endpoints of triangles over filling, storing the excess in the hole.

Bake with 8 coals underneath and 18 coals on the lid for 20 to 25 minutes or until golden brown.

You can do the same thing with a 375-degree home oven. When it is mid-January and 10 degrees outside on my deck, I cook in my kitchen oven.

Serve with sour cream and salsa.

Cheeseburger Casserole

Whenever we have a neighborhood potluck dinner, we throw this together in one of our backyards. You can do the whole thing in a 12-inch oven, or brown the meat, onions, and bell pepper at home in a frying pan before you go. Other than the burger, cheese soup, and potatoes, everything is replaceable. We have tried almost every veggie and cheese available. It can become an amazing creation with a mind of its own.

12-inch oven
8 coals underneath and 16 on the lid
350 degrees in your home oven

2 pounds 85% hamburger
1 medium yellow onion, half sliced and half diced
1 bell pepper, chopped or sliced as thin as you like
1 medium head of broccoli, cut so you only use the florets
1 (10-oz.) can condensed cheese soup
1 (16-oz.) bag frozen hash brown potatoes, thawed to room temperature
1 tsp. kosher salt and black pepper
other shredded cheeses (optional)
bacon bits (optional)
sour cream (optional)

Brown the meat halfway and drain most of the juice. Add the onion and bell pepper and finish cooking the meat until done. Stir in broccoli and cheese soup. Spread the potatoes evenly over the top; season with salt and pepper. Cook with 8 coals underneath and 16 coals on the lid for 30 minutes. When it starts to bubble, pull 4 coals from underneath the pot and place on the lid for 10 minutes to brown the potatoes.

We often put out bowls with several types of shredded cheese, like mozzarella or cheddar, so people can top their own dish with their favorite cheese. Try sour cream and bacon bits.

Serves 10

Dad's Chinese Pudding

When I was about 12 years old, my father arrived home from work with a recipe for something he called Chinese Pudding that a coworker had given him. We had a large family (6 children), so he liked one-pot meals. This one fit the bill nicely. We never did understand why it was called Chinese Pudding. However, the name stuck, and we still call it that today. My siblings and their children still cook this dish.

12-inch oven
8 coals underneath and 16 on the lid
350 degrees in your home oven

2 lbs. hamburger, browned and crumbled, drained
4–5 lbs. potatoes, mashed, recipe below
1 stick butter, sliced into 8 pieces (cut in half, then half of that, etc.)
9 (¼-inch) Velveeta cheese slices
2 packages frozen corn, thawed and at room temperature

Spray a Dutch oven with nonstick cooking spray. Spread ⅓ of the potatoes on the bottom of the pot. Place 3 slices of the cheese evenly on the potatoes. Place pats of butter in between the cheese slices. Spread ½ of the hamburger over the cheese. Spread ½ of the corn over the hamburger. Repeat for layer number 2.

Now you have ⅓ of the mashed potatoes, 3 slices of the cheese, and 2 pats of butter remaining. Spread the potatoes on top. Arrange the cheese evenly. Dot remaining pats of butter and place them between the cheese slices.

Cook for 30 minutes with 8 underneath and 16 coals on the lid. In your kitchen oven, bake at 350 degrees for about 30 minutes. It's hard to overcook this dish, so don't worry too much about the time. The best way to check this dish the first time you prepare it is to literally dig into it with the serving spoon. When the cheese is melted, it's ready.

Serves 10 (at least it did in the 1960s). Options: I occasionally add a chopped onion or a chopped bell pepper to the hamburger as it is frying, depending on who's coming for dinner.

Mashed Potatoes

4–5 lbs. potatoes
1 stick butter, room temperature
½ teaspoon salt
⅛ teaspoon black pepper
½ cup sour cream
milk

Peel, quarter, and boil the potatoes. Drain, add the salt and pepper, and mash or run through a potato ricer. Combine with the butter, sour cream, and enough milk to make a creamy consistency. Start with ¼ cup milk and go from there.

Easy Enchilada Casserole

This tastes like enchiladas, but is a casserole-style you can serve with a spoon individually for a group. I did this for some election judges on election day several years ago. There were zero leftovers. It can be doubled using a 12-inch oven or even tripled using a 14-inch oven.

10-inch oven
7 coals underneath and 14 on the lid for a 10-inch oven
350 degrees in your home oven

2 lbs. 85% lean ground beef
12 corn tortillas
1 (4-oz.) can chopped olives
1 (10-oz.) can cream of chicken soup
1 (10-oz.) can cream of mushroom soup
1 (10-oz.) can cream of celery soup
1 large sweet onion, sliced or diced
1 lb. shredded cheddar cheese, usually 2 (8-oz.) bags
1 (4-oz.) can diced green chiles (optional, as these are quite spicy)
1 (10-oz.) can enchilada sauce
sour cream, guacamole, and salsa

Place 8–10 coals underneath a 10-inch oven and brown the beef in batches until well done. Remove with a slotted spoon and drain. Drain the excess grease from the oven and return the beef.

Add the cheese, soups, enchilada sauce, olives, onion, and chiles one at a time, incorporating each one before adding the next ingredient. Cut corn tortillas into strips or 2-inch sections (I just tear them up with my hands) and fold into the mix.

Bake for 50–60 minutes at 350 degrees. It will be bubbling, especially around the edges.

Garnish with sour cream, guacamole, and salsa.

Serves 5–6

My Dad's Enchiladas

This is another one pot meal from my dad. I realized when I was an adult with my own children why he liked this type of meal. You can feed six kids with 36 of these. He used the broiler pan from the kitchen oven. We'll do 12 here. You can double the recipe with a 14-inch oven, but use only one more can of chili.

12-inch oven
8 coals underneath and 16 coals on the lid
350 degrees in your home oven

1 lb. 85% lean hamburger
1 large onion, diced
(Velveeta) cheese, 3 (¼-inch) slices (cut each slice into 4 equal strips, 1 per enchilada)
1 dozen corn tortillas
corn oil
2 (14-oz.) cans of chili, any kind

Brown the burger and the onions in a large frying pan. When meat is totally browned, drain and set aside to cool. In a 10-inch (or so) skillet, heat about ½ cup corn oil.

Using tongs, fry one tortilla in the oil for about five seconds on each side. If the tortilla starts to bubble up and harden, you've fried it too long. Keep it limp. Note: The tortilla will be very hot after it is fried. I keep a small bowl of ice water nearby or leave the cold water trickling in the kitchen sink to cool my fingers. You'll learn fast how to handle them.

Using the tongs, place the tortilla on a flat surface like a cutting board and place two tablespoons burger/onion mix and one strip cheese on the tortilla. Roll it up and place in a 12-inch oven seam-side down.

My wife Vickie and I do this as a team, one frying the tortillas and one rolling. Guess who does the rolling?

Repeat until all the enchiladas are layered in the pot. Add the leftover hamburger to the chili and pour over the enchiladas. You can also spread some of your favorite grated cheese on top.

Put 8 coals underneath and 16 coals on top and cook 30 minutes. Yum! Or preheat your kitchen oven to 400 degrees and lower to 350 when you add the pot.

Top with your favorite hot sauce.

Serves 4 with 3 per portion

Italian Meatloaf

I always wear rubber gloves mixing meatloaf to make hand-washing easier.

12-inch oven
8 coals underneath and 16 on the lid
350 degrees in your home oven

1 lb. 85% lean hamburger
1 lb. Italian sausages, hot or not, sliced
1 cup panko crumbs
2 eggs
1 cup sliced button mushrooms (buy the packaged ones at the store)
1 Tbsp. minced garlic
½ medium onion, finely chopped
¼ tsp. ground oregano
1 cup any bottled spaghetti sauce, divided

Mix together ½ cup of the spaghetti sauce with the rest of the ingredients and combine by hand. Don't overmix; it will turn into a hockey puck.

Place in a loaf pan to shape it and transfer to a trivet in a 12-inch oven. Cook for 30 minutes with 8 coals underneath and 16 on the lid. Brush on the remaining ½ cup spaghetti sauce and cook with 8 underneath and 18 coals on top until the coals are dead, 60 minutes. Serve with your favorite side dishes. We like mashed potatoes and gravy and canned green beans.

Serves 8–10

Italian Meatballs

This recipe goes with many different types of pasta, from spaghetti to macaroni.

12-inch oven
8 coals underneath and 16 on the lid
350 degrees in your home oven

2 lbs. 85% fat hamburger
½ cup finely diced onion
1 egg
1 tsp. salt
½ tsp. ground oregano
1 Tbsp. Worcestershire sauce
1 bottle of your favorite spaghetti/pasta sauce

In a mixing bowl, combine all of the ingredients. Don't overmix. I always wear rubber gloves when mixing ground meat to make cleanup easier.

Form the mixture into small balls with a #50 ice cream scoop (page X), about golf-ball size.

Brown them in a large skillet, cook for 4–5 minutes per side, and place in the Dutch oven.

Add enough sauce to cover the meatballs and bake for 50–60 minutes with 8 coals underneath and 16 coals on top until the coals are about dead.

Serve over pasta or rice.

Serves 6–8

Mexican Hamburger Pie

As you will see, this recipe can be modified many ways according to individual tastes. Remember, the easier way is to read this recipe and line up all of the ingredients on the counter before you make it. BTW: It tastes as good the second day as leftovers! Kind of like real thick chili with soggy chips.

12-inch oven
8 coals underneath and 16 on the lid
350 degrees in your home oven

2 lbs. 85% lean ground beef
1 large onion, diced
1 green pepper, sliced or diced
½ tsp. salt
2 Tbsp. chili powder
1 tsp. pepper, fresh-ground (if you have it)
1 Tbsp. minced garlic (I get mine from a jar)
1 (14.5-oz.) can of diced tomatoes
2–3 (15-oz.) cans chili, your choice of flavor
1 (14.5-oz.) can corn
8 oz. grated cheese, your choice
1 (11-oz.) bag of Doritos chips, your choice of flavor
sour cream (optional)
shredded lettuce (optional)

Brown ground beef with onions, green pepper, and salt. Drain thoroughly and stir in chili powder, ground pepper, and garlic.

While you are browning the burger, stir the tomatoes in a separate bowl with the chili, corn, and about half of the cheese. Add beef/onion/garlic/green pepper mix. Adjust spices to taste. Season with salt and pepper if needed.

In a large mixing bowl, crush the chips with your hands and spread about half in the bottom of a 12-inch Dutch oven. Pour in hamburger pie mixture, top with rest of the Doritos, and cook for approximately 30–40 minutes with 8 coals underneath and 16 coals on the lid, around the edge. If you are using your kitchen oven, preheat to 375 degrees and drop to 350 when you put in the Dutch oven.

Sprinkle remaining cheese on top during the last 5 minutes of cooking. You can garnish each serving with some sour cream, lettuce, and extra cheese; maybe some hot sauce, too.

Serves 8

Oriental Casserole

For a chow mein feel with Westernized ingredients, this dish uses hard noodles and soft, much like what you will find in Chinese restaurants in the U.S.

12-inch oven
8 coals underneath and 16 on the lid
350 degrees in your home oven

2 Tbsp. butter
3 stalks celery, diced
1 medium yellow onion, diced
1 bunch green onions, rough-chopped
8 oz. sliced mushrooms
2 cups hard chow mein noodles, divided
2 cups (about 8 oz. dry) cooked and drained soft rice noodles (you can use vermicelli)
meat: 1 lb. round steak, diced, and then pan-fried, or
          1 lb. pork loin, sliced, diced, and then pan-fried, or
          2 boneless, skinless chicken breasts, cooked and shredded (or 4–5 boneless,
              skinless thighs, cooked and shredded,
          or some of each
1 green pepper, rough-chopped
1 (10-oz.) can cream of celery soup
¼ tsp. black pepper
1 cup chopped cashews (optional)

Melt the butter in the Dutch oven with 8 coals underneath. Add the celery, mushrooms, and onion and cook for a few minutes. Add 1 cup hard noodles, the rice noodles, and your chosen meat. Stir until combined. In a large bowl combine remaining ingredients, season to taste, and pour over the noodle mix.

Evenly spread the remaining chow mein noodles on top. Bake at 350 degrees for 30 to 40 minutes, with the same 8 coals underneath and 16 coals on the lid.

Remember, you can simply put your Dutch oven in your kitchen oven. Just preheat to 375 and reduce the temperature to 350 when you put the Dutch oven on the rack.

Serves 8

Porcupine Meatballs Deluxe

12-inch oven
8 coals underneath and 16 on the lid
350 degrees in your home oven

2 lbs. 85% lean hamburger
1 cup minute rice
1 medium onion, diced
1 bell pepper, diced small
1 egg
1 tsp. seasoned salt
4 cups vegetable juice (your favorite house brand is okay)
½ tsp. ground cinnamon
¼ tsp. ground nutmeg
2 Tbsp. sugar (or raw honey if you have it)
2 Tbsp. Worcestershire sauce

In a mixing bowl, combine the rice, the hamburger, ½ cup of the diced onion, ½ cup of the diced green pepper, egg, and salt. Put any excess vegetables in the Dutch oven. Most bell peppers equal about ½ cup when diced small.

Heat the vegetable juice, remaining bell pepper and onion, cinnamon, nutmeg, sugar, and Worcestershire sauce in a 12-inch oven over 12 coals for about 10–15 minutes (or on the stove for about 10 minutes if you are cooking at home—you want it to be just past warm).

Form the hamburger mix into small balls with a #50 ice cream scoop, a little bigger than a golf ball. Brown them 4–5 minutes in a big skillet and add to the oven with the sauce.

Cook for 50–60 minutes using 8 coals underneath and 16 coals on top and until the coals are about dead. In your kitchen oven, preheat to 375 and turn down to 350 when you put the oven on the rack. Cook for 50–60 minutes.

Serve over rice or any pasta. Or maybe make a sandwich on a sub roll; use the extra sauce for dipping the sandwich.

Serves 8–10

Stuffed Meatloaf

This is really great for Sunday backyard family gatherings.

12-inch oven

2 lbs. 85% lean hamburger
1 cup bread crumbs—panko, if you have it, or just crush up some saltine crackers
1 egg
1 tsp. onion powder
½ tsp. garlic powder
½ tsp. black pepper
1 tsp. salt
½ cup of your favorite BBQ sauce

Filling
8 oz. cream cheese, softened
1 medium onion, finely diced
½ cup finely chopped mushrooms (optional)
(you can put almost any vegetable in the filling that you like)

Topping
1 Tbsp. Dijon mustard
1 Tbsp. brown sugar
¼ cup ketchup

In a large mixing bowl, combine the meatloaf ingredients. I do this with my hands. Don't over-mix; it will be way too dense. Lightly flour your cutting board (or any flat surface) and pat out the meatloaf mix into a 9 by 13 rectangle. Spread the cream cheese filling evenly over the rectangle. Roll up using a pastry cutter (or anything that will help you roll it). Gently place on a round trivet in a 12-inch oven.

Cook for 30 minutes with 18 coals on top and 10 underneath.

Lift the lid, brush on the topping, and cook for 30 more minutes. Check temperature with a meat thermometer and cook for ten minutes more until it reaches 160 degrees. Let it rest for 10 minutes while you finish your side dishes.

Cut into 1-inch slices with a serrated knife and serve with any potato dish and a veggie.

Serves 8–10

Stuffed Peppers

Many years ago I started to cook stuffed peppers this way because I always had trouble with the meat cooking and the peppers were never cooked through. We never went back to the "cut the top of the pepper off, scoop out the seeds, and fill the hole with meatloaf mix" version. The seeds and ribs are much easier to remove this way, too.

12-inch oven
10 coals underneath and 18 on the lid
350 degrees in your home oven

Meatloaf
2 lbs. 85% lean hamburger
1 cup panko crumbs or 6 saltine crackers, crushed with your hands
1 egg
½ tsp. black pepper
1 tsp. salt

4 big bell peppers, cut in half lengthwise and seeded

Topping
2 Tbsp. brown sugar
¼ cup ketchup

In a large mixing bowl, combine the meatloaf ingredients. I do this with my hands.

Fill each green pepper half with meatloaf mix.

Arrange in a 12-inch Dutch oven. Use a round trivet if you have one.

Cook for 30 minutes with 10 coals underneath and 18 coals on the lid.

Lift the lid, brush liberally with the topping, and cook for 15 more minutes.

Serves 8

Sweet-and-Sour Meatloaf with BBQ Dipping Sauce

The balance between sweet and vinegar is highlighted here by the maple syrup and vinegar. Try switching the maple with strawberry or raspberry syrup. This is a great main dish recipe when you have family over for Sunday dinner. Enjoy!

12-inch oven
8 coals underneath and 16 on the lid
350 degrees in your home oven

Meatloaf
2 lbs. 85% lean ground chuck
1 any color bell pepper, seeded and chopped
½ small onion, diced
¾ cup panko bread crumbs
½ cup Parmesan cheese
¼ cup maple syrup
¼ cup red wine vinegar
2 eggs

BBQ Dipping Sauce (in an 8-inch oven or medium saucepan)
1 green bell pepper, finely chopped
1 small white onion, diced small
¼ cup brown sugar
1 teaspoon dry mustard
1 teaspoon fresh lemon thyme (or ¼ cup lemon juice)
½ cup ketchup
¼ cup dark molasses
¼ cup soy sauce
2 tablespoons red wine vinegar
pinch of kosher salt
powdered chili peppers or cayenne pepper to taste

Mix all the ingredients together. Don't overmix. Load it into a loaf pan, cover with plastic wrap, and refrigerate for 30 minutes.

Put a round trivet in a 12-inch Dutch oven, put a loaf-size piece of parchment or foil on it, and gently invert the loaf pan on it.

Remove the loaf pan.

Bake with 16–18 coals on top and 8–9 underneath until internal temperature reaches 160 degrees, about 1 hour. Check temperature around 40 minutes, and then every 10 minutes. Coals are good for about 1 hour.

Remove and let it sit, covered with foil, for 15 minutes. When you cut it, cut in half, then each piece in half again, and so on. Use a serrated bread knife to serve.

Try with fluffy mashed potatoes and steamed broccoli.

Serves 8

Three-Cheese Tater Tot Casserole

One cheese casseroles are boring. If you line everything up on your counter first, this goes together in about 2 minutes.

12-inch oven
8 coals underneath and 16 on the lid
350 degrees in your home oven

1 lb. 85% lean hamburger
1 medium onion, diced
salt and pepper
2 cans cream of anything soup
2 cups milk
½ cup vegetable juice
1 (16-oz.) bag mixed veggies
1 (8-oz.) bag shredded medium or sharp cheddar cheese
1 small container Parmesan cheese, any brand
2 tsp. garlic salt
1 Tbsp. mustard powder
1 (32-oz.) bag tater tots, divided
1 (8-oz.) bag shredded pepper jack cheese

Brown ground beef and onion in a 12-inch oven. Season with salt and pepper. Add soup, milk, vegetables, cheddar and Parmesan cheese, and all of the seasonings. Stir until combined. Gently fold in a little more than half of the tater tots. Top with the rest of the tots and sprinkle with the pepper jack cheese. Cook for 45–50 minutes with 8 coals underneath and 16 on the lid. Serve immediately.

Serves 8

Vickie's Weekday Hamburger Casserole

This is a family favorite for many years. It was handed down from my wife Vickie's grandmother. I modified it for Dutch ovens.

12-inch oven
8 coals underneath and 16 on the lid
350 degrees in your home oven

2 lbs. 85% lean ground beef
1 large yellow onion, sliced thin
1 (15-oz.) can green beans (note: avoid the cheap ones that often have pieces of stem)
2 cans condensed tomato soup
salt and pepper
5 medium potatoes
½ lb. cheddar cheese, sliced

Break up the ground beef in a 12-inch Dutch oven and cook with the onion over 12 coals until the meat is no longer pink. Drain and return to the oven. Stir in green beans and soup and season with salt and pepper, about ¼ teaspoon each. Boil the potatoes and mash. Spread on top of the hamburger mix. Lay the cheese slices on top. Cook for 30 minutes with 16 coals on the lid and 8 underneath, or bake at 350 degrees in your home oven for 30 minutes. Preheat the oven to 400 and drop to 350 when you add the pot.

Serves 12

Bacon Cheese Potatoes with Meatballs

For years we made the bacon cheese potatoes as a side dish. Then one afternoon we noticed some pre-cooked meatballs in the cooler at the store. We added them to the potatoes and made it a one-pot meal. It's great favorite comfort food to fill the grandkids' tummies! If they don't like onions and bell peppers, don't add them.

12-inch oven
10 coals underneath and 14 on the lid
350 degrees in your home oven

1 lb. any bacon
4 large potatoes, diced to ½-inch
1 medium onion, diced
1 bell pepper chopped any way you want
8 oz. cheese, your choice
1 package Italian meatballs, uncooked (Walmart has these)

Dice and fry the bacon with 10 coals underneath the oven, just short of crisp. Drain on paper towels and return to the oven. Discard about half of the bacon grease, add the potatoes, onions, and peppers, and stir. Arrange the cheese and meatballs on top and cook with the same 10 coals underneath and 14 coals on the lid until the coals are about dead, 50–60 minutes.

Serves 8

Bacon Bomb

This dish looks hard to do, but it is really very easy—just get all of the ingredients on the counter before you start. Then all you have to do is reach and add. Many versions of this recipe use seasoned sausage, but I don't think that is necessary. This looks so good, it will amaze everyone who sees it! Building the lattice is a snap when you know how! Just Google "bacon lattice" for dozens of YouTube video tutorials.

12-inch oven
10 underneath and 20 coals on the lid
425 in your home oven

1 lb. thick-cut bacon, divided
2 lbs. ground pork, room temperature
8 oz. cream cheese, room temperature
1 medium onion, sliced thin
1 bell pepper, sliced or diced or both
bottle of your favorite BBQ sauce

Cut four pieces of bacon into ½-inch pieces and fry to your preference. Set aside on paper towels to drain.

Lay a sheet of parchment paper on your counter and place the ground pork in the middle. Spread with your hands until you have about a 12 by 12–inch square (about ½-inch thick). Spread the cream cheese over left half of the pork and add the bacon bits, onions, and bell peppers. Liberally brush with BBQ sauce and gently roll it up with a pastry cutter from the cream cheese side. Set aside.

Make a 5 by 5 lattice with 10 pieces of bacon. It's way easier than you might think. Place the pork roll with the seam toward you on the edge of the lattice closest to you. You want the seam to end up on the bottom when you bake it. Roll it on the bacon, picking up the lattice as you go.

Brush liberally with BBQ sauce. Cook on a Dutch oven trivet for about 60 minutes at 425 degrees, with 10 coals underneath and 20 coals on the lid. Check with a meat thermometer at 50 minutes and then every 10 minutes until it reaches 150 degrees. Brush one more time with BBQ sauce and continue cooking for 10 more minutes. When it's done, let it sit for 10 minutes so it can set up.

Serves 8

Bacon Cheddar Dutch Oven Lasagna

This bacon-laced lasagna will warm the heart of all bacon lovers. If it seems like a lot of work, that's okay; family and friends make it all worthwhile. Remember, line everything up on the counter before you assemble it.

12-inch oven
8 coals underneath and 16 on the lid
350 degrees in your home oven
(if you are using your kitchen oven, preheat to 400 degrees)

1 lb. cottage cheese
2 eggs
½ cup grated Parmesan cheese
8 oz. grated cheddar cheese
12 oz. packaged bacon, diced cold in the package
1 medium onion, diced
1 lb. 85% ground chuck
1 (24-oz.) bottle Italian sauce (like Ragú)
1 (14.5-oz.) can diced tomatoes (don't drain—the noodles need the water)
1 lb. (2 8-oz. bags) grated mozzarella cheese
1 box oven-ready lasagna noodles

In a medium bowl, combine the cottage cheese, eggs, Parmesan, and cheddar. Set aside. Dice the bacon into ½-inch pieces in the package and dump into a cold 12-inch oven.

Put 12 coals underneath and fry until barely crisp. Remove with a slotted spoon and drain on paper towels. Discard half of the bacon drippings. Add the beef and onions. Cook until meat is browned. Use a slotted spoon to transfer the hamburger to a large mixing bowl with the bacon, and then add the Italian sauce and tomatoes and mix until combined.

To assemble this dish, evenly spread 1 cup of the sauce in the bottom of a 12-inch Dutch oven.

Evenly arrange 3 of the noodles on the sauce. You may need to break them to fit the round shape of the pot. That's okay; it doesn't have to be pretty. Spread half of the cottage cheese mix over the noodles. Add ⅓ of the sauce and smooth it out over the cottage cheese mix. Spread about ⅓ of the grated mozzarella cheese over the sauce.

Lay out 3 more noodles, the remaining cottage cheese, another ⅓ of the sauce, and another ⅓ of the mozzarella. Arrange another 3 noodles on top. Top with the remaining sauce and mozzarella cheese. You could add some more cheddar here.

Cook with 8 coals underneath and 16 coals on the lid for 45 minutes. Remove the coals and let it rest with the lid off for 10 minutes. If you use your home oven, preheat to 400 and drop to 350 when you put the pot in.

Serves 8 (but I am never really sure; it goes so fast!)

Bacon Manicotti

I always thought that this dish was too hard to build to be a favorite until I discovered the zip-lock bag trick. Once you get the sauce together, you are set. It isn't real pretty in the pot, but this recipe is one of our top ten family favorites. The neighbors loved it.

12-inch oven
10 coals underneath and 14 on the lid
350 degrees in your home oven

Filling
1 (16-oz.) tub ricotta cheese
2 Tbsp. pork dry rub
1 egg
1 (3-oz.) bottle real bacon bits

Sauce
1 (24-oz.) can pasta sauce, your choice
2 (14-oz.) cans diced tomatoes, Italian flavor (or not)
1 Tbsp. honey (you can substitute sugar)
1 tsp. salt
1 (8-oz.) box manicotti shells (14 shells)
8 oz. bag shredded Italian cheese mix

Combine the filling ingredients and set aside.

Pour the sauce ingredients into a 12-inch oven and stir.

Spoon the filling into a zip-lock bag, cut off a corner, and stuff the manicotti shells. Place in the oven and add just enough water to cover the shells. Sprinkle the shredded cheese over the whole thing.

Cook with 10 coals underneath and 14 coals on the lid for 1 hour, until about the time when the coals die.

Serve with Easy White Rolls (page 16).

Serves 8

Easy Ham and Cheese Noodle Casserole

I'm a fan of one-pot meals because they take less time and cleanup is easy. I like egg noodles because the store-bought version is quick and easy to serve.

12-inch oven
8 coals underneath and 16 on the lid
350 degrees in your home oven

12 oz. bag egg noodles
nonstick cooking spray for the oven
cheese sauce (recipe below)
2 cups diced ham—I buy a small ham steak and dice it up
8 oz. shredded cheese, your choice

Cheese Sauce
1 can condensed cheddar cheese soup
½ cup buttermilk
½ cup sour cream
2 cups broccoli florets
1 medium onion, half diced and half sliced thin
1 bell pepper, any color, chopped small
½ cup (two stalks) celery, diced small
1 Tbsp. butter
1 (8-oz.) package sliced mushrooms, rinsed and drained

Cook noodles in lightly salted boiling water to al dente, about 4–5 minutes. Drain in a colander and rinse with cold water to stop the cooking. Set aside.

Start the sauce by combining soup, milk, sour cream, and broccoli in a medium bowl. Set aside. While the noodles are boiling, sauté the onions, peppers, celery, and mushrooms in 1 tablespoon butter for a few minutes in a medium skillet and add to the bowl. Stir in ham.

Pour everything into a sprayed 12-inch Dutch oven. Bake with 8 coals underneath and 16 coals on the lid around the edge for 40 minutes. Remove from coals, evenly spread the shredded cheese on top of the casserole, and put the lid back on for 5 minutes.

If you like a little heat, add a tablespoon or two of Sriracha sauce for a nice kick.

Serves 8

Chicken and Potatoes

You can change several things in this recipe, including quantities (leave room at the top for the chicken), types of vegetables, and which cream-of-something soup.

12-inch oven
8 coals underneath and 16 on the lid
350 degrees in your home oven

4 lbs. chicken pieces, your choice, seasoned with salt and pepper
½ stick butter
6 russet potatoes, peeled (or not) and sliced to ½-inch
4 ribs celery, sliced, diced or chopped
1 yellow onion, sliced, diced or chopped
2 green or red bell peppers, sliced, diced, or chopped
8 oz. sliced button mushrooms (I buy them presliced)
2 cans cream-of-something soup

Preheat your oven with 10 coals underneath. Cut the butter into three or four chunks and add to the oven. Move it around until it melts and starts to bubble. Add the chicken and brown for 2 minutes per side, turning once. Remove the chicken and set aside. Add the vegetables and stir to coat. Add the cans of your favorite cream-of-something soup, right on top. Cut (or don't) the chicken any way you like and put on the top of the vegetables.

Put 8–10 coals underneath and 14–16 around the outside of the lid and then just leave it alone until the coals are almost dead, 60 minutes.

Serves 6–8

Chicken Enchiladas

12-inch oven
8 coals underneath and 16 on the lid
350 degrees in your home oven

1 package flour tortillas (usually 10)
2 medium boneless, skinless chicken breasts, chopped, or 3 (5-oz.) cans chicken, drained
5 (¼-inch) slices Velveeta cheese, sliced in half
2 Tbsp. butter
1 bell pepper, chopped
1 rib celery, sliced thin on the bias
1 medium onion, diced
2 bottles of Alfredo sauce (or your favorite cheese sauce)
8 oz. cream cheese, room temperature
1 small head broccoli, chopped
1 cup shredded cheese, your choice
Sriracha sauce (optional)

Melt the butter in a 12-inch oven with 10 coals underneath and sauté the bell pepper, celery, and onion until softened, 3–4 minutes. Remove and set aside. Add ½ cup Alfredo sauce and spread evenly.

Break up the chicken in a mixing bowl and add the sautéed onion–pepper mix. Lay a flour tortilla on your cutting board, place ¼ cup chicken mix with a slice of melty cheese in the middle, and roll up. Place seam side down in pot.

Repeat 9 more times.

While you are sautéing the veggies, add the remaining Alfredo sauce, cream cheese, and broccoli to a smaller pot or saucepan. Cook over low heat until it's warm and the cream cheese is melted, but not boiling.

Pour over enchiladas, squirt some Sriracha sauce (optional) over the cheese sauce, and top with shredded cheese.

Cook for 30 minutes with 8 coals underneath and 16 coals on the lid. In your kitchen oven, preheat to 400 and drop to 350 when you put the pot in the oven. This recipe is easy to double in a 14-inch pot, except you only need a total of 3 bottles Alfredo sauce.

Serves 8–10

Cream of Anything Chicken and Veggies

This recipe is a great way to look like an accomplished Dutch oven cook on your first try! Great for backyard dinners with friends and family! You can change several things in this recipe, including quantities (leave room at the top for the chicken), types of vegetables, and which cream-of-something soup. Browning the chicken at the beginning (the flesh will turn white) just firms it up a bit so it doesn't slide around if you decide to cut it. Plus, it adds some chicken flavor to the butter. The chicken can be cut just before you add it to the veggies—or not at all. Enjoy!

12-inch oven
8 coals underneath and 16 on the lid
350 in your home oven

4 boneless, skinless chicken breast halves, seasoned with salt and pepper
½ stick butter
4 ribs celery, sliced, diced, or chopped
1 yellow onion, sliced, diced, or chopped
1 red onion, sliced, diced, or chopped
2–3 green or red bell peppers, sliced, diced, or chopped
8 oz. sliced button mushrooms
1 can cream-of-something soup
5 (¼-inch) slices melty cheese (Velveeta)
½ cup cream cheese

Preheat your oven with 12 coals underneath.

While the oven is heating, prepare the vegetables and set aside in a big bowl. Cut the butter into three or four chunks and add to the oven. Move it around until it melts and starts to bubble.

Add the chicken breasts and brown for 2 minutes per side, turning once. Remove the chicken and set aside. Add the vegetables and stir to coat. Cut (or don't) the chicken any way you like and put on the top of the vegetables. Add a can of your favorite cream-of-something soup, right on top. Place the melty cheese and dollops of cream cheese on top and put the lid on. Put 8 coals underneath and 16 around the outside of the lid, and then just leave it alone until the coals are almost dead.

Serves 6–10

Mom's Egg Foo Yung

From Indonesia to China, this dish is fairly universal, although every country does it a bit differently. This recipe is our family version and has been a favorite for many years.

12-inch oven
8 coals underneath and 16 on the lid
350 degrees in your home oven

15 eggs, beaten
½ cup vegetable oil
1 tsp. each salt, black pepper, and garlic powder
2 Tbsp. butter
1 medium onion, diced
4 ribs celery, sliced very thin
1 cup chopped button mushrooms
1 (16-oz.) can bean sprouts, drained
3 green onions, chopped thin
½ cup fresh parsley, minced
1 cup diced ham or 2 cans salad shrimp, drained

In a large mixing bowl, beat the eggs with the oil and spices.

In a large skillet, melt 2 tablespoons butter and sauté the onion, celery, and mushrooms for 5 minutes. Cool to room temperature. Add everything to the eggs and stir well.

Spray a 12-inch Dutch oven with nonstick spray and pour in the egg foo yung mixture.

Bake with 8 underneath and 16 coals on top until the eggs set, 30 minutes.

You can bake this in your kitchen oven. Preheat to 375 and drop it to 350 degrees when you put the Dutch oven on the rack.

Serves 6

Ham Fried Rice

This recipe came from an Air Force friend who had spent time in Korea back in the '90s. It's not too complicated and tastes just like Chinese restaurant fried rice. Use the best soy sauce you can find for the best result. Serve as a side for a big meal or the main dish for lunch.

12-inch oven
12 coals underneath, bottom heat only

2 cups uncooked long-grain white rice
4 cups water
2 Tbsp. butter
2 Tbsp. vegetable oil
1 small onion, chopped
1 bell pepper, chopped
1 Tbsp. minced garlic (I buy mine in a jar—much easier)
1 (8-oz.) bag frozen peas or mixed vegetables
2 cups diced ham
4 eggs, beaten and seasoned with black pepper
a dash of red pepper flakes for the eggs (optional)
soy sauce, the very best you can find at your local Asian store
1 tsp. Worcestershire sauce (optional)

It's easy if you remember the main steps: 1) cook the vegetables, add the ham, and stir; 2) make a well in the mix and scramble the eggs; and 3) add the rice and stir.

The night before you make this dish, cook rice according to package directions and refrigerate in an airtight container overnight. It will make about 6 cups.

Heat butter and oil in a 12-inch oven over 12 coals or at medium-high on your kitchen stove.

Stir in bell pepper and onion and cook for 5 minutes. Add garlic and cook for 1 minute.

Add vegetables and cook for 5 minutes. Add ham and cook for 1 minute. Make a well in the middle and pour in beaten egg. Cook until scrambled. Mix it to break up the eggs. Add rice and combine. Stir in just enough soy sauce to make it light brown.

Squirt some Worcestershire sauce on the finished dish for a slightly sweeter taste.

Serves at least 6—it doesn't last long

Jambalaya

This is adapted from Carl Rasmussen's famous recipe. It looks like a lot of work, but despite the long list of ingredients, it is quite easy to prepare and well worth the effort! If you line the ingredients up before you start, preparation is a snap!

12-inch oven
12 coals underneath, bottom heat only
(you can also cook this recipe on a propane stove on medium heat)

4 oz. (1 stick) butter
1 large white onion, sliced thin
2 stalks celery, chopped thin
1 green bell pepper, sliced thin
1 red bell pepper, sliced thin
1 Tbsp. minced garlic (I get mine from a jar—much easier)
2 boneless, skinless chicken breasts, sliced into 1-inch pieces
½ lb. smoked sausage, sliced into ½-inch pieces
½ lb. hot Italian sausage, sliced into ½-inch pieces
½ cup diced ham
2 (14- or 15-oz.) cans diced tomatoes
2 cups long-grain rice
1 tsp. oregano leaves
½ tsp. thyme leaves
1 tsp. black pepper
1 tsp. Cajun seasoning
½ tsp. Cayenne pepper
1 (32-oz.) box low-sodium chicken broth
1 lb. precooked medium shrimp

Melt the butter with 12 coals under the oven. Add the onions, celery, peppers, and garlic and stir until the vegetables are well coated. Cook for 5 minutes until the onions are a bit wilted.

Add the chicken and cook for 5 minutes, stirring occasionally. Stir in sausages, ham, and tomatoes. Add the rice and stir in the seasonings. Add the chicken broth and bring to a boil. After the mixture begins to boil, remove 6 coals from under the oven.

Simmer with the lid on for 30 minutes, stirring once or twice. Fold in the shrimp and cover again. Wait five minutes and serve.

Serves 10–12 as a side dish or 6–8 as a main dish

You can change the texture and size or the amounts of the ingredients to create your own version.

Cheese Noodles with Meatballs

It's nice to switch to egg noodles once in a while, and cheese matched with meatballs is a great combination. Try to have everything at room temperature before you start.

12-inch oven
8 coals underneath and 16 on the lid
350 degrees in your home oven

1 Tbsp. butter
1 Tbsp. flour
up to 2 cups milk, divided
1 tsp. mustard powder
½ tsp. basil
½ tsp. oregano
1 tsp. parsley flakes
1 (8-oz.) bag shredded cheddar cheese
salt and pepper to taste
½ cup milk
1 (8-oz.) bag wide egg noodles
1 (1-lb.) bag precooked turkey meatballs
1 cup white cheese, shredded, any kind

Melt the butter in a medium saucepan and stir in flour. Cook for a few minutes until it forms a light roux. Slowly add 1 cup milk and cook until you get a nice white sauce, 5 minutes. If it's too thick, add a few extra teaspoons of milk. Add the herbs and the cheddar cheese and season with salt and pepper. Stir in ½ cup milk and add the noodles. Add the meatballs and cook with 8 coals underneath and 16 coals on the lid for 30 minutes. Sprinkle the white cheese over the top and replace the lid just long enough to melt the cheese, 5 minutes.

Serves 8

Bacon Mac and Cheese and Cheese

This is a great side dish when several families get together while up on the mountain. We kicked it up with the bacon and two cheeses. Sometimes we add ½ cup Parmesan to the topping.

12-inch oven
8 coals underneath and 16 on the lid
350 degrees in your home oven

1 lb. elbow macaroni
1 lb. bacon, diced and fried
½ cup panko breadcrumbs
1 Tbsp. extra-virgin olive oil
¼ tsp. dried rosemary, or your favorite herb, minced
4 cups (32 oz.) milk, divided
½ cup flour
4 cups (32 oz.) shredded cheddar cheese, sharp or not
1 pint (16 oz.) small-curd cottage cheese
¼ teaspoon salt
⅛ tsp. fresh ground pepper, with my pepper mill it's 20 twists
2 tsp. mustard powder

Add the pasta to lightly salted boiling water and cook for 7–8 minutes until al dente. Drain in a colander and rinse in cold water to stop the cooking. Set aside.

Chop the bacon into ½-inch pieces in the package, remove the plastic, and fry over medium heat, 10 coals, in a 12-inch oven until just crispy. Drain on paper towels. Discard the grease.

While the bacon is frying, mix breadcrumbs, oil, and rosemary in a small bowl. Set aside.

Heat 3 cups milk in the (still warm) oven over medium-high heat until simmering, but not boiling. Stir remaining 1 cup milk with flour in a small bowl and whisk into the hot milk.

Simmer on medium-low heat, whisking constantly, until the sauce thickens. Remove from heat and stir in the shredded cheese until melted. Stir in cottage cheese, salt, and pepper. Add half of the bacon and mix well. Fold in the cooked pasta and evenly sprinkle the breadcrumb mix over the top.

Bake for 30 minutes with the lid on with the same 10 coals underneath. It should be bubbling gently around the edges. If not, leave it on the coals for a few more minutes; you want everything to be melted.

Serves 8

Barbecue Chicken Pizza

If you want the absolute easiest way to prepare this, go to your local pizza shop and buy a premade pizza dough ball. It tastes almost as good and cuts the preparation time in half.

12-inch oven
10 coals underneath and 20 on the lid
425 degrees in your home oven

Dough
1 cup warm water
2 Tbsp. vegetable oil
3–4 cups bread flour
1 package instant yeast
1 Tbsp. sugar
1 tsp. salt

Filling
1 cooked, store-bought rotisserie chicken, boned
¾ cup barbecue sauce, your choice
1 cup shredded mozzarella cheese
½ cup medium or sharp cheddar cheese
½ onion, sliced very thin

To prepare the dough, add the water and oil to a large mixing bowl. In another bowl, combine flour with yeast, sugar, and salt. Add 1 cup of this mix to the water and stir vigorously for at least 30 seconds. Slowly add more flour mix 1 cup at a time until it starts to pull away from the sides of the bowl. Knead it on a lightly floured board for 5 minutes. When it gets a bit rubbery, cover and let sit for 30 minutes to rise and hydrate. Roll out to a 12-inch circle and place in a 12-inch oven. Move it around with your hands and about ½ inch up the sides.

While the dough is rising, bone the chicken with your hands. You want ½-inch or so pieces. Add to a large mixing bowl. Spread about ¼ cup of sauce on the dough, add the rest of the sauce to the chicken, and toss until the chicken is coated.

Spread the mozzarella cheese on the dough, add the chicken, and top with the cheddar and onions. Cook with 10 coals underneath and 20 coals on the lid until the crust starts to brown, 20–25 minutes. Let it sit with the lid off for 5 minutes before serving.

Serves 6

Pork Lover's Deep-Dish Pizza

As with many of the pizzas I make in a Dutch oven, I buy a dough ball from the local pizza place. It saves time and makes the backyard cooking easier. If you want to make it from scratch, the dough recipe is here.

12-inch oven
10 underneath and 20 coals on the lid
425 degrees in your home oven

Dough
¾ cup warm water
2 Tbsp. vegetable oil
2–3 cups bread flour
1 package instant yeast
1 Tbsp. sugar
1 tsp. salt

Filling
½ cup pizza sauce of your choice
8 oz. shredded mozzarella cheese
2 oz. sliced ham
2 oz. sliced pepperoni
½ lb. bacon, diced and cooked
1 green pepper, diced
1 small red onion, diced
4 oz. sliced mushrooms, sliced some more
4 oz. can sliced black or green olives, drained
½ cup shredded monterey jack/cheddar mix cheese

To prepare the dough, mix the water and oil in a large mixing bowl. In another bowl, combine 1 cup flour with yeast, sugar, and salt. Add 1 cup of this mix to the water and stir vigorously for at least 30 seconds. Slowly add more flour mix ½ cup at a time until it starts to pull away from the sides of the bowl. Knead it on a lightly floured board for 5 minutes. When it gets a bit rubbery, cover and let sit for 30 minutes to rise and hydrate. Roll out to a 12-inch circle and press into a 12-inch oven with your hands, plus 1 inch up the sides.

Evenly spread the pizza sauce on the dough. Next, the mozzarella cheese. Next, the meats. Add the vegetables and mushrooms. Finally, sprinkle on the monterey jack cheese.

Cook with 20 coals on the lid and 10 underneath until the crust starts to brown, 20–25 minutes. Flip it over and let sit for 5 minutes before slicing to serve.

Serves 8

Sweet and Sour Pork Meatballs

We bought some of these premade meatballs on a whim, and of course we just had to try them in the Dutch oven. They turned out to be quite delicious.

12-inch oven
10 coals underneath and 14 on the lid
350 degrees in your home oven

2 (1-lb.) packages premade pork meatballs, about 2 dozen (Walmart has these)
1 Tbsp. butter
1 Tbsp. canola oil
1 Tbsp. minced garlic
1 bell pepper, any color, sliced
1 large sweet onion, sliced
4 oz. sliced mushrooms
½ cup packed brown sugar
1 cup ketchup
¼ cup vinegar
2 Tbsp. soy sauce
1 Tbsp. Worcestershire sauce
2 Tbsp. cornstarch in ½ cup water

Put meatballs in a cold Dutch oven and place over 12 coals. Cook, turning occasionally, for 10 minutes. Remove to a plate and add butter and oil to the oven. Heat the oil and add the pepper slices, onion slices, and garlic. Sauté for 8 minutes and add the mushrooms. Cook for 1 more minute and add the ketchup, vinegar, soy sauce, and brown sugar. Stir in the cornstarch slurry and cook until it thickens. Return the meatballs, cover, and add 12 coals to the lid. Cook for 20 minutes.

Serve over any pasta or rice.

Serves 6–8 with 3 or 4 meatballs per serving

Pork Chop One-Pot Dinner

My grandchildren, Kendrick and Samantha, won the youth division with this dish at Utah's Weber County Fair Cook-off in 2008. You can cook this dish in your home oven: Preheat to 375 degrees and reduce to 350 when you put the Dutch oven in the kitchen oven. The cooking time is the same.

12-inch oven
8 coals underneath and 16 on the lid
350 degrees in your home oven

4 potatoes, peeled (or not) and thick-sliced
1 green bell pepper, sliced or diced or both
1 red bell pepper, sliced or diced or both
1 large onion, sliced or diced or both
1 Tbsp. butter
4 big pork chops, seasoned with salt and pepper
5 ears of fresh corn broken in half
1 can of cream-of-something soup
¼ cup bacon bits

Cut the potatoes, bell peppers, and onions. Put them in a big bowl and set aside.

Spray the inside of a 12-inch Dutch oven with nonstick cooking spray. Preheat the Dutch oven with 10 coals underneath. Brown the pork chops for 30 seconds per side, then remove and set aside.

Arrange the half-ears of corn vertically in a circle around the sides of the oven. Fill the remaining space with the potatoes, peppers, and onions.

Scoop the can of soup on top. It won't be on top very long because it melts into the vegetables.

Sprinkle the bacon bits on top. Arrange the pork chops on top of that.

Put the lid on and cook with 14 coals on the lid, around the edge, along with the 10 already underneath. Cook for 50–60 minutes.

Serves 4 with 1 chop each

You can change several things in this recipe, including types of soup or veggies.

Sausage and Potato Casserole

10-inch oven
7 coals underneath and 14 on the lid
350 degrees in your home oven

1 lb. hot (or not) Italian sausages
2 Tbsp. butter, divided
1 Tbsp. vegetable (canola) oil
1 medium onion, sliced or diced or both
2 stalks celery, chopped thin
4 medium potatoes, diced (I do this with a French fry cutter)
1 tsp. minced garlic (I get mine from a jar)
1 (14.5-oz.) can diced tomatoes, Italian-style (don't drain)
1 cup frozen peas
4 oz. shredded cheddar/jack cheese

Slice the sausage casings, remove the sausage, and cut into 1-inch pieces.

In a 10-inch Dutch oven, melt 1 tablespoon butter with 10 coals underneath. Cook sausage, onion, and celery in oil over medium heat until sausage is no longer pink. Remove to a mixing bowl with a slotted spoon.

Drain all but 1 tablespoon fat and add the other tablespoon butter. Add potatoes and cook, stirring occasionally, until they are fork tender, about 10 minutes.

Stir in garlic and cook for another minute.

Return the sausage and vegetables to the oven and add the tomatoes and peas. Cook with the same 10 coals underneath and 14 new coals on the lid for 30 minutes.

Sprinkle the cheese on top and serve.

Serves 4

Easy Zucchini Bacon Cheese Tomato Bake Dinner
(Sometimes with Mushrooms)

In late summer every year I'm overrun with zucchini, some of which has been hiding and has grown quite large. We also grow tomatoes, and we buy a lot of bacon (since it is a main food group around here), so we make this dish through October.

10-inch Dutch oven (if you only have a 12-inch oven, just add 50% more ingredients)
350 degrees in your preheated kitchen oven (preheat to 375)

1 (12-oz.) package bacon, diced to 1 inch
3 cups diced fresh zucchini, about 2 medium
       Cut the seeds off, dice, and soak in saltwater for 20–30 minutes. Rinse well.
1 cup sliced mushrooms
3–4 cups fresh chopped tomatoes, or 2 (14-oz.) cans diced tomatoes
½ cup Parmesan cheese
kosher salt
black pepper
1–2 cups shredded cheese, your choice

Cut bacon into 1-inch pieces and fry in a large frying pan to just before crisp. Remove with a slotted spoon and set aside on paper towels to drain.

Discard half of the drippings; add the zucchini and sauté until barely soft, then transfer it into a 10-inch Dutch oven with the slotted spoon.

Add the bacon, mushrooms, tomatoes, and Parmesan cheese. Season with the salt and pepper.

Top with the shredded cheese and cook for 30 minutes with 14 coals on the lid, around the edge, and 7 underneath, around the edge.

Or, if you prefer, preheat your home oven to 400, pop it in, and lower the temperature to 350 degrees for 30 minutes.

Serves 3–4 (or, as a side dish, 6–8)

Vickie's Famous Sweet and Sour BBQ Chicken

My wife Vickie dreamed up this recipe to feed the grandkids one Easter. If you cook this on your stove, start with medium-high heat to brown the chicken and turn down to medium-low to finish it off. This is way easier than it looks, because each of the sauce main ingredients is ½ the volume of the previous one: 2 cups ketchup, 1 cup brown sugar, ½ cup molasses, ¼ cup soy sauce, 2 tablespoons vinegar, 1 tablespoon lemon juice (easy to remember).

12-inch oven
8 coals underneath and 16 coals on the lid
350 degrees in your home oven

Chicken
2 Tbsp. butter
6–7 boneless, skinless chicken breast halves, as many it takes to cover the bottom of the oven

Sauce
1 green bell pepper, chopped or sliced
1 red bell pepper, chopped or sliced
1 yellow bell pepper, chopped or sliced
1 white onion, chopped or sliced fine
1 red onion, chopped or sliced fine
2 cups ketchup
1 cup brown sugar
½ cup molasses
¼ cup soy sauce
2 Tbsp. red wine vinegar
1 Tbsp. lemon juice
1 Tbsp. dry mustard
1 tsp. oregano
1 tsp. fresh ground pepper
1 Tbsp. minced garlic (I get mine from a jar)
salt to taste

Start with about 30 coals in a chimney starter. While they are getting ready, cut the vegetables and set aside. When the coals are ready, put 10 coals underneath the oven. Add the butter, let it sizzle a bit, and add the chicken. Brown on each side for 2 minutes, just until it turns a bit white. Set aside. Add the vegetables and the sauce ingredients to the oven and lay the chicken breasts on top of the veggies—or you can cut the chicken into to 1-inch pieces and stir it in.

Cover and cook with the same 10 coals underneath and 16 coals on top. Cook about 15 minutes, then reduce number of coals on top to 14. Cook for 30 more minutes. Remove from the heat and let it cool down for a few minutes with the lid on.

Serve with rice. We like to add ½ cup diced onion to the rice when we cook it. Add it about halfway through the cooking.

Serves 10

Many main dishes profit from a matching side dish to enhance the meal. Three of these are for big sporting events like the Super Bowl, where you have a crowd.

Chapter 5: Sides

Baked Corn

10-inch oven
7 coals underneath and 14 on the lid
350 degrees in your home oven

1 package corn muffin mix
1 (15-oz.) can corn, drained
1 (15-oz.) can creamed corn
1 green bell pepper, diced small
½ cup sour cream
4 oz. (½ package) cream cheese, room temperature
4 oz. (1 stick) butter, melted

Spray 10-inch oven with nonstick cooking spray. Add a parchment ring (page XI) and spray again.

Mix together all ingredients and pour into oven.

Bake with 7 coals underneath around the edge and 14 coals on the lid around the edge for about 50–60 minutes, until the coals are about dead.

If you use your kitchen oven, preheat to 400 and reset to 350 when you put the pot in the oven.

You can add bacon bits or sausage and/or onions.

Serve as a side dish for 8–10 people

Cheese Hors d'Oeuvres

We make these for many big sporting events, such as the Super Bowl. You can easily double or triple the recipe using a larger Dutch oven.

12-inch oven
8 coals underneath and 16 on the lid
350 degrees in your home oven

2 cans refrigerator rolls (Pillsbury® Grande)
8 oz. cheddar cheese, cut into 1 inch pieces
½ cup butter, melted
¼ cup garlic bread crumbs

You can do this in your home oven—preheat to 400 degrees and lower to 350 when you add the Dutch oven.

Spray 12-inch oven with cooking spray. Cut the cheese into ¾-inch pieces and set aside.

Remove dough from each can and cut into 16 pieces: 2-4-8-16. Roll out each piece and wrap around a piece of cheese, making sure to seal cheese completely inside dough. Dip each one into melted butter and coat with bread crumbs. Place in oven, beginning in the middle.

Cook for 30 minutes with 8 coals underneath and 16 coals on the lid.

Check at 25 minutes, and when the rolls are golden brown, pull the coals. Leave the lid on for a few minutes, then transfer to a serving platter. Make some dipping sauce from the sauce section of this book and enjoy.

Serves a small sports crowd

Hasselback Potatoes

This is a fancy way to serve what are basically baked potatoes. Except these are extraordinary!

12-inch oven
8 coals underneath and 18 on the lid
375 degrees in your home oven

6–8 russet baking potatoes
½ cup (1 stick) room temperature butter
oregano or your favorite herb
½ cup grated cheese, any kind
kosher sea salt

Place a wooden spoon on your cutting board and position the potato against it. Slice into the potatoes about ⅛ inch apart. Do not cut completely through (the wooden spoon will help).

Spray a 12-inch Dutch oven with nonstick spray and add as many cut potatoes as you can, maybe 7 big russets. Top each potato with ½ tablespoon of butter and a pinch of herb and bake with 8 coals underneath and 18 coals on the lid for 40 minutes.

Remove the lid and sprinkle each potato with kosher salt and cheese.

Top each potato with a ½ tablespoon of butter again.

Replace the lid and bake for another 20 minutes until the coals are about dead.

To bake in your home kitchen oven, preheat to 425 degrees. When you put the Dutch oven in, drop the temperature to 375.

Serve with any meat dish.

Serves 1 potato per person

Spicy Baked Cauliflower

I saw this several times online and decided to put my spin on it in a Dutch oven. It works quite well. This is a good side dish for most meals. If you like spicy foods, use more chili powder.

12-inch oven
9 coals underneath and 18 on the lid
375 degrees in your home oven

1 head cauliflower
1 Tbsp. vegetable oil
2 (6-oz.) containers plain Greek yogurt
2 Tbsp. chili powder
1 Tbsp. cumin
1 Tbsp. garlic powder
1 tsp. lime juice
1 tsp. kosher salt
½ tsp. black pepper

Spray a 12-inch oven with cooking spray. Insert a parchment ring (page XI) and spray that too.

Trim the base of the cauliflower to remove any green leaves and the woody stem.

In a medium bowl, combine all of the ingredients. Use a brush or your hands to smear the mixture over the cauliflower. Place the cauliflower in the oven and cook, with 9 coals underneath and 18 coals on the lid, for 40 minutes until the surface is dry and lightly browned. Let the cauliflower cool for 10 minutes with the lid on and serve as a side dish.

Refrigerate the extra mix for up to a week. It's great as marinade to preseason meat for grilling.

If you use your kitchen oven, preheat to 425 and lower to 375 when you add the Dutch oven.

Serves 6–8

Steamed Cabbage

We did this for years in a steamer basket. It is one of the easiest sides you can do in a hurry, and cabbage is inexpensive. Try various toppings like bacon, sausage, butter, oil and vinegar, salt and pepper, or hard grated cheese. We like just the bacon with butter, salt, and pepper.

1 lb. thin bacon, diced small
1 head cabbage, your choice, green or red or even savoy or napa
salt and pepper
butter
olive oil (optional)
cider vinegar (optional)
anything else in the intro above

Dice and fry bacon in a 12-inch oven; set aside on paper towels to drain. Discard the bacon grease. (Some Southern recipes will save the drippings and drizzle over the cabbage.) Put a trivet in the oven and add 2 cups water. Start 12 coals and evenly place them underneath the oven.

Cut cabbage into quarters, cut out the cores, and discard any bad outside leaves. Season all sides with salt and pepper. As soon as the water boils, put the cabbage quarters on the trivet cut-side down and place the lid on the oven. When it boils, cook for 15–20 minutes or more, depending on your preference. We like it a bit soggy, around 25 minutes. When it's ready, remove with tongs to a serving plate, top with bacon and your favorite stuff, and serve with or without a main dish because if you put enough bacon or sausage on it with a little cheese you have a main dish.

Serves 4 or 8 if you cut each quarter

Super Bowl Lil' Smokies

The hard part with this recipe is wrapping each of the little sausages with the bacon. It is well worth the 10 minutes it takes to do this. You can easily double this recipe with the same 12-inch oven. Sometimes I will grind some black pepper over them just before I cook them. Our Super Bowl crowd thought these were quite yummy!

12-inch oven
8 coals underneath and 18 on the lid
375 degrees in your home oven

1 lb. bacon, slices cut into thirds in the package
4 oz. (1 stick) butter, melted
2 cups dark brown sugar

Wrap each piece of sausage with a piece of bacon, stick a toothpick in it, and place it into a 12-inch oven. Melt the butter and add one cup brown sugar. Pour evenly over the sausages. Sprinkle the other cup of brown sugar over this. Cook for 30 minutes with 8 coals underneath and 18 on the lid. If the bacon isn't quite done, put the lid back on for a few more minutes.

I serve these right out of the pot, but you can get fancy and place them on a serving platter. They seldom last long enough in a crowd to get to a platter.

Super Bowl Wings and Thighs

We have these with the Lil' Smokies (from the previous page) at every Super Bowl and other sporting events—like the NBA Finals, the World Series, the Stanley Cup playoffs, Sunday night football, and so on. The mighty black pot greatly enhances the flavor.

12-inch oven
8 coals underneath and 18 on the lid
375 degrees in your home oven

1 lb. chicken wings
1 lb. skinless chicken thighs
1 cup barbecue sauce, your choice
¼ tsp. fresh ground pepper
Sriracha sauce or any good hot sauce (optional)

Add all of the ingredients to a 12-inch oven, cover, and cook for 45–50 minutes.

Serve hot with a bottle of hot sauce on the side.

Serves 6

Easy Sweet Pepper Pasta

We like pasta and often substitute macaroni dishes for potatoes. This pasta dish is adapted from a recipe by Pioneer Woman Ree Drummond. It's one of my favorites when I'm in a hurry and need a quick side dish.

12-inch oven
8 coals underneath and 16 on the lid
350 degrees in your home oven

8 oz. pasta, your choice
2 Tbsp. virgin olive oil
1 Tbsp. butter
½ sweet onion, sliced thin
1 Tbsp. minced garlic
½ tsp. oregano leaves
1 (16-oz.) jar roasted red peppers, don't drain
1 cup beef broth
big pinch salt
¼ tsp. black pepper
½ cup sour cream
1 cup Parmesan cheese, divided

Add pasta to boiling water and cook for 10 minutes. Drain and set aside.

Add olive oil and butter to a 10-inch oven with 10 coals underneath and heat.

Add the onions, garlic, and oregano and sauté for 3 minutes.

Add red peppers and simmer for 5 minutes.

Spoon into a food processor and purée for 30 seconds.

Pour the purée back into the oven. Add the broth, salt, and pepper, and cook until reduced by about a third. Add the sour cream and mix well.

Stir in Parmesan and pasta and put the lid on until ready to serve.

Serves 6–8 as a side dish

I was first introduced to desserts at the feet of Grandma. She made cakes, pies, and cookies of all kinds. Over the course of my growing up, I ate thousands of oatmeal cookies, which I found out much later were simply made from an oatmeal box recipe, slightly modified for the grandkids.

Raisins in some, nuts in others; all complimented by cold milk.

Everyone likes a sweet ending to a good meal. These 12 recipes are from my personal favorites.

Most of them allow for experimentation by using slightly different ingredients.

Remember that Dutch oven cakes are essentially cold oven cakes, where you start with a cold oven and bake longer. Most of them allow for experimentation by using slightly different ingredients.

Chapter 6: Desserts

Apple Raisin Upside-Down Cake

We all like apples and raisins, and the nutmeg seals the deal.

10-inch oven
7 coals underneath and 14 on the lid
350 degrees in your home oven

Filling
4 Tbsp. unsalted butter
½ cup firmly packed light brown sugar
½ cup raisins
½ tsp. cinnamon
⅛ tsp. nutmeg
2 Granny Smith apples, peeled and thinly sliced

Cake (the easy variation here is a boxed cake mix)
6 tsp. soft unsalted butter
1 cup sugar
3 eggs, room temperature
1 tsp. vanilla extract
2 cups unbleached flour
3 Tbsp. cornmeal
2 tsp. baking powder
1 tsp. baking soda
1 tsp. salt
1 cup buttermilk

Spray a 10-inch oven with nonstick cooking spray.

Combine the butter, sugar, raisins, cinnamon, and nutmeg in a small saucepan and bring to a boil for 30 seconds. Take off the heat and stir in the apples.

Pour this mixture into the oven and spread evenly.

To make the cake, beat the butter and sugar together with a wooden spoon for two minutes.

Add the eggs and vanilla and beat until very smooth, about 2 more minutes.

Add the flour, cornmeal, baking powder, baking soda, and salt, and beat 10 seconds.

Pour in the buttermilk and stir just until combined.

Gently pour the batter over the apple/raisin mixture.

Bake 50 minutes, or until a knife inserted in the center of the cake comes out dry.

Run a knife along the outer edge of the cake to loosen it from the oven.

Let the cake cool and turn it out onto the lid.

Serves 8

Vickie's Apple Crisp Surprise

I call this dish a surprise because it looks a bit different each time I make it.

10-inch Dutch oven
7 coals on bottom and 14 coals on the lid
350 degrees

Apples
2 Tbsp. butter, melted
1 cup sugar
⅛ tsp. freshly ground nutmeg
1 tsp. cinnamon
8 tart apples, peeled, cored, and thinly sliced

Topping
1 cup Bisquick
½ cup brown sugar
1 tsp. cinnamon
3 Tbsp. cold butter, cut into ½-inch cubes
½ cup rolled oats

In a large bowl, combine butter, sugar, and spices. Add the apples, stir to coat, and dump into Dutch oven.

In a medium bowl, combine Bisquick, oats, brown sugar, and cinnamon. Cut in the butter with your hands; there is no need to keep it cold like a pie crust. Spread this mixture over the apples, making sure it is spread all the way to the edges.

Cover and bake, using 7 coals underneath the oven and 14 coals on top, for 40 minutes.

After 20 minutes of baking time, take the 7 coals from underneath the oven and place them on the lid, inside the existing ones, and then bake for another 20 minutes. Check after the 40 minutes (total) are up—the top should start to crisp up nicely. When it does, discard all of the coals and let it sit for 5 minutes with the lid off. Let it cool completely. This is good served with whipped cream, nuts, and/or Caramel Sauce (page 113).

Serves 10–12

Banana Upside-Down Cake

The brown sugar and butter preclude using a parchment ring—it won't stick.

12-inch oven
8 coals underneath and 16 on the lid
350 degrees in your home oven

1 cup brown sugar
6 Tbsp. butter, about ¾ of a stick, cut into small pieces
6 bananas, peeled and sliced lengthwise
1 (12-oz.) bottle maraschino cherries without stems, drained
2 boxes yellow cake mix
2 tsp. banana flavoring

Spread the brown sugar and small pieces of butter in the bottom of Dutch oven.

Press the bananas flat-side down into the brown sugar and butter. Sprinkle the cherries over the bananas.

Prepare the cake mixes according to box directions, stir in the flavoring, and carefully pour over the fruit.

Cover and bake, using 8 coals underneath and 16 coals on the lid, for 45 minutes. Check at 40 minutes by inserting a table knife in the center of the cake, and if not done, add 10 more minutes. Let it cool for 20 minutes and flip the oven over, serving the cake from the lid.

Serves 8–10

"Cast iron careth not from whence the heat cometh" (Me, about 1998). You can do this in your home oven when it's 10 degrees outside on your deck. Preheat to 375 degrees and drop to 350 when you add the Dutch oven.

Easy Raisin Bread Pudding

Great for breakfast. You can make this the day before.

12-inch oven
8 coals underneath and 16 on the lid
350 degrees in your home oven

4 eggs, beaten
2 cups milk
2 tsp. vanilla
½ tsp. salt
¼ cup brown sugar
1 (15-oz.) can fruit, your choice
½ cup raisins
6 cups bread (the drier the better), cubed, about ¾ loaf

Whisk together eggs, milk, vanilla, salt, and brown sugar in a large mixing bowl.

Stir in fruit (with the juice) and raisins and then fold in the bread. Cover and refrigerate for several hours or overnight to soak the bread.

When you are ready to bake it, spray a 12-inch oven, add a parchment ring (page XI), spray that too, and pour in the mixture.

Cook about 45 minutes with 8 coals underneath and 16 on the lid.

Let it rest for 10 minutes and serve warm with one of the sweet sauces in chapter 7 or whipped cream.

Refrigerate leftovers for several days.

Serves 10

Chocolate Banana Marble Cake

We cooked this at a church gathering and it was so well received we added it to our favorites list.

12-inch oven
8 coals on bottom and 16 coals on top
350 degrees

Cake
1 box chocolate cake mix
1 box white cake mix
        (each cake mix requires 3 eggs, water, and vegetable oil)
5 bananas

Frosting
1 (8-oz.) package cream cheese, room temperature
½ cup (1 stick) unsalted butter, room temperature
1 tsp. vanilla
3 cups powdered sugar
2 Tbsp. milk
½ tsp. salt

Mix all frosting ingredients together in a medium bowl, cover, and set aside while you bake the cake.

Mix each cake in its own bowl according to box directions. Slice a banana into ¼-inch slices and fold into each mix. Spray Dutch oven generously with cooking spray. Place a parchment paper ring in the bottom of the oven and spray it too. Pour the chocolate cake batter into the oven first. Next, drop big tablespoons of the white cake batter in a circle and one in the middle on top of the chocolate cake mix. Now, stick a spoon into each white puddle until it hits the bottom of the oven and turn—don't stir. Gently pour the rest of the white cake mix on top.

Cover and bake, using 8 coals underneath the oven and 16 coals on top, for 45 minutes. Every 15 minutes, gently turn the oven about a quarter-turn over the coals, and then turn the lid the opposite direction to prevent hot spots. After 45 minutes, poke the cake with a long toothpick or a table knife to test for doneness. The toothpick should come out clean. If not, bake few more minutes. When done, the cake will shrink away from the sides of the oven.

Transfer it to a cooling rack and cool to room temperature. When it cools down, slice it in half horizontally with a serrated knife. Flip the top half over onto the lid and cover with half of the frosting.

Cover with ¼-inch slices of bananas, about 2 bananas. You can also double the bananas here. Place the other half of the cake on top, cut-side down. Spread the remaining frosting on the top of the cake and refrigerate for several hours to set the frosting.

Serves 10–12

Cherry Chocolate Cobbler

This cobbler batter tends to blend with the cherries on the bottom, giving it a cherry cake look. Pour in the batter very carefully!

10-inch oven
7 coals underneath and 14 on the lid
350 degrees in your home oven

2 cups flour
½ cup sugar
½ cup nuts, your choice, finely chopped (optional)
1 Tbsp. baking powder
½ tsp. salt
½ cup (1 stick) butter, room temperature
1 (8-oz.) package semi-sweet chocolate chips
½ cup milk
1 egg
1 (15-oz.) can dark pitted cherries

Melt the chocolate in a metal bowl over hot (not boiling) water. Remove from heat and cool slightly. While you are waiting for the chocolate to melt, combine dry ingredients and butter in a large bowl with your hands. Set aside. In a smaller bowl, whisk milk, cherry juice, and egg together and add to melted chocolate. Blend chocolate mixture into flour mixture.

Place a parchment paper ring in the bottom of a 10-inch oven and add drained cherries. Spoon batter carefully over cherries.

Bake at 350 degrees with 7 coals underneath, around the edge, and 14 coals on the lid for 35–40 minutes.

Check with toothpick and add time if not done.

Serve warm with whipped cream or fruit sauces; many good options can be found in chapter 7.

Serves 6–8

Raspberry Pecan Pie

I made this at a kitchen store demo and it was amazing to watch it disappear. It's a straightforward, simple recipe that you can easily change by switching the syrup flavor. We have tried many pecan pies and this one is our favorite. My family and friends tell me it is to die for.

10-inch oven
12 coals underneath and 20 coals on the lid
450 degrees in your home oven (starting temperature)

1 cup raspberry syrup
1 cup packed light brown sugar
½ cup heavy cream
1 Tbsp. dark molasses
4 Tbsp. (½ stick) butter, cut into small pieces
½ tsp. salt
7 large egg yolks, whisked for 10 seconds
2 cups pecan halves

If you use your kitchen oven for this pie, preheat to 450 degrees.

Heat syrup, sugar, cream, and molasses in a medium saucepan over medium heat, stirring occasionally until sugar dissolves, about 3 minutes. Remove from heat and whisk in butter and salt until the butter melts. Let it cool for 10 minutes and whisk in egg yolks until incorporated. You don't want scrambled eggs.

Place parchment paper lifts (see page XII) in the oven, spray them, and evenly place the pie shell in the oven, about 1 inch up the sides.

Scatter pecans in pie shell. Carefully pour filling over. Bake with 9 coals underneath and 18 coals on the lid for 15 minutes. Be sure to place the coals around the edges only.

After 15 minutes, remove 6 coals from the lid and 4 from underneath the oven. Continue cooking for 50–60 minutes. Check at 50 minutes. When the center of pie still jiggles a bit, pull the coals. Let it cool with the lid off until it sets.

Carefully transfer it to a rack with the parchment paper lifts to finish cooling to room temperature. Refrigerate for several hours. Bring to room temperature before serving.

When baking in your kitchen oven, preheat to 450 degrees for at least 30 minutes. Place the Dutch oven on the center rack for 15 minutes. Then, carefully remove the lid and reduce the temperature to 325 degrees.

Bake until filling is almost set and center jiggles slightly, 50–60 minutes. Put the lid on for a few minutes and then remove the pie. Cool pie on rack for 1 hour and refrigerate several hours. Bring to room temperature before serving.

Serves 6

Rice Pudding

Every cookbook has a recipe for rice pudding . . . This is my Dutch oven version. This recipe works well on the stovetop or on a camp stove.

2 cups uncooked white rice
5 cups milk, divided
1 cup white sugar
¾ tsp. salt
3 eggs, beaten
2 cups golden raisins (or 1 cup raisins and 1 cup chopped dates)
3 Tbsp. butter
2 tsp. vanilla extract

Bring 4 cups water to a boil in a 10-inch oven; stir rice into boiling water. Reduce heat to low, cover, and simmer for 20 minutes. I usually cook the rice the night before and refrigerate overnight in an airtight container. This allows the rice to fully absorb any water.

In a 10-inch oven, combine the cooked rice and the sugar. Add 4 cups milk, sugar, and salt.

Cook over medium-low heat on your kitchen stove until thick and creamy, 15–20 minutes. Stir in remaining 1 cup milk, beaten eggs, and raisins; cook until the eggs set, stirring constantly. Remove from heat and stir in butter and vanilla.

Makes 6 cups

Strawberry-Kiwi Boston Cream Pie

When we want to get fancy at the neighborhood potluck dinner or a big family event, we do this dish in the morning and refrigerate until it's time to eat.

12-inch oven
8 coals underneath and 16 on the lid
350 degrees in your home oven

Cake
2½ cups flour
1½ cups sugar
2 tsp. baking powder
1 tsp. baking soda
¼ tsp. nutmeg
1 tsp. salt
½ cup vegetable oil
¾ cup buttermilk, divided
2 eggs
1 teaspoon vanilla
2 kiwifruits, peeled and sliced
1 small (8-oz.) jar strawberry glaze
16 oz. (1 lb.) sliced strawberries

Filling
2 egg yolks
¾ cup sugar
2 Tbsp. cornstarch
1 cup milk, divided
1 tsp. vanilla
1 Tbsp. unsalted butter

In a large bowl, combine the flour, sugar, baking powder, baking soda, nutmeg, and salt. Whisk together the oil, vanilla, and ½ cup buttermilk. Add the eggs and remaining buttermilk. Spray a 12-inch oven with nonstick cooking spray and add a parchment paper ring; spray the ring and gently pour in the batter.

Cover and bake, using 8 coals underneath the oven and 16 coals on top, for 40 minutes. Every 15 minutes, gently turn the oven about a quarter-turn over the coals, and then turn the lid the opposite direction to prevent hot spots. Near the end of baking time, poke the cake with a long toothpick or a table knife to test for doneness. The toothpick should come out clean. If it's still a bit wet, just put the lid back on for 10 minutes. When done, let it rest with the lid off for 10 minutes, then turn cake out onto the lid and cool to room temperature.

While the cake is baking, make the filling. Whisk together yolks, sugar, cornstarch, vanilla, and 2 tablespoons milk in a small bowl. Bring remaining milk to a simmer in a small skillet or saucepan. Quickly whisk about ¼ cup hot milk into the eggs. Slowly add this yolk mixture to the hot milk in a slow stream, whisking constantly until it starts to thicken. Whisk in butter, pour into a bowl, and cover with plastic wrap. Cool to room temperature.

When the cake and the filling are cooled, carefully split the cake in half horizontally with a serrated knife. Spread the filling and the kiwifruit slices on the bottom half. Place the top half on the filling cut-side down and spread the strawberry glaze evenly over the top. Arrange the sliced strawberries in the glaze. Spread more glaze over the strawberries. Serve with whipped cream, if desired.

Serves 8

Three Fruit Upside-Down Swirl Cake

We have made this cake for many years because it is easy and foolproof. The boxed cake mixes ensure anyone can make a great dessert. I can have the whole family over for this one.

12-inch oven
8 coals underneath and 16 on the lid
350 degrees in your home oven

1 German chocolate cake mix
1 white cake mix
1 (14-oz.) can each of your three favorite fruits (drain and reserve juice)

Mix each cake separately according to box directions. You can substitute some of the fruit juice for an equal amount of water called for in either mix, about ¼ cup each. Spray a 12-inch oven generously with nonstick spray, add a parchment ring (page XI), and spray that too. Arrange fruit in the bottom of the oven.

Gently pour the German chocolate cake mix right on the fruit and spread it evenly. Next, drop big tablespoons of the white cake mix on the chocolate batter. Now stick the spoon into each puddle until it hits the bottom of the oven. Don't stir. Pour the rest of the white mix on top.

Cook for 50 minutes with 8 coals underneath and 16 coals on the lid before you look the first time.

When it looks solid, check with a table knife. If it's not done, check every 10 minutes until the knife is clean.

Let it cool with the lid off. When it cools down, put the lid back on, run a kitchen knife around the edge, and flip the oven over. The cake will come out on the lid.

Serves at least 10

Simple Rustic Fruit Tart

You can make this wonderful dessert with a storebought crust and one can of any fruit filling. This is the easiest pie in the world to make.

12-inch oven
8 coals underneath and 16 on the lid
350 degrees in your home oven

1 frozen pie crust, carefully thawed to room temperature
1 (20-oz.) can fruit pie filling; the most common are apple, cherry, blueberry, and peach
⅛ tsp. nutmeg
½ tsp. cinnamon
1 Tbsp. raw sugar or dark brown sugar

Spray a 12-inch oven and place three parchment paper lifts (see page XII) equally around the bottom, spraying each one as you add it.

Carefully place a premade pie crust in the middle and press it 1 inch up the sides. Pour a canned fruit pie mix in the crust and fold it over the fruit.

Combine ⅛ teaspoon nutmeg, ½ teaspoon cinnamon, and 1 tablespoon sugar in a small bowl and sprinkle over the top.

Cook with 10 coals underneath and 20 coals on the lid for 30 minutes. Check it and continue to bake until the crust is golden brown and the filling is bubbling. Pull it from the oven using the parchment handles with three people. You can do it with two if you are careful.

Serve warm with vanilla ice cream or a flavor to match the fruit.

Serves 8

Very Berry Pizza

The truth is that I use premade pie crusts when I cook for family. They think this is just fine. If you have high-end company like your mother-in-law (bless her heart) coming over, follow the crust recipe from scratch.

12-inch oven
8 coals underneath and 16 on the lid
350 degrees in your home oven

Crust
1 cup warm water
2 Tbsp. vegetable oil
3–4 cups bread flour
1 package instant yeast
1 Tbsp. sugar
1 tsp. salt

Filling
1 (8-oz.) package cream cheese
½ cup brown sugar
½ tsp. vanilla
1 (15-oz.) tub frozen sliced strawberries
2 cups blueberries
3 kiwifruits, thinly sliced

Combine the crust ingredients in a large bowl. Mix with your hands until the dough forms a smooth ball. Flatten ball into a 1-inch-thick disc, place in a large zip-lock bag, and chill for at least 1 hour. Press the dough into the bottom of a 12-inch oven with your hands. Cover and bake, using 6–8 coals underneath the oven and 14–16 coals on top, for 35–40 minutes until the crust is done. Let it cool completely, turn it out of the oven, and put it on the lid.

While it is cooling, mix the cream cheese, brown sugar, and vanilla until smooth. Evenly spread this over the crust. Arrange the fruit any way you want and refrigerate the whole thing for at least one hour; three or four hours is better.

Serves 8

Chapter 7: Sauces, Toppings, and Frostings

Apple Pecan Topping

Serve warm with ice cream. One big tablespoon per serving should do it. Try with pancakes and waffles. If you run out of ice cream, you can refrigerate for up to a week.

10-inch oven
13 coals on the lid and 6 underneath

¼ cup (½ stick) butter, sliced into small pieces
1 cup brown sugar, divided
3 apples, peeled, cored, and diced small
1 (10- to 12-oz.) package pecan pieces
½ cup golden raisins, chopped a bit
¼ cup flour
½ tsp. ground cinnamon
⅛ tsp. ground nutmeg
juice from one orange, plus some of the zest
1 tsp. vanilla extract

Evenly place the butter pats around the bottom of a 12-inch oven. Sprinkle ½ cup of the brown sugar over the butter. Mix the rest of the ingredients together and spread over the brown sugar.

Bake for 45–50 minutes (until the coals are about dead) with 14 coals on the lid and 8 underneath.

If you use your kitchen oven for baking in your Dutch ovens, preheat to 375 and lower to 350 when you put in the oven. When done, stir it for a few seconds with a wooden spoon.

Apricot Glaze

This glaze is meant for pork, from chops and ground pork dishes to roasts.

1 (15-oz.) can apricots, drained and coarsely chopped
½ cup honey
½ tsp. kosher salt
6 jalapeños, seeded and minced (wear gloves!)

Mix ingredients together and simmer in a small pot for 10 minutes, continuously stirring.

Remove from heat and let cool a bit with the lid off.

Banana Chutney

Keep it as simple as possible, without the Indian flair normally associated with chutneys. You don't need South Asian spices flavoring this recipe. The only ingredient that should remain constant is the bananas. Adjust the lemon juice and honey to your taste. Try grating some of the zest from the lemon into the mix while it's cooking.

5–6 very ripe bananas
½ cup raisins
¼ tsp. salt
1 Tbsp. lemon juice, about one medium lemon
1 Tbsp. honey
4 oz. cream cheese (½ package)

Peel the bananas, slice them, and put them in a medium saucepan. Add the raisins and smash with a potato masher. Add the lemon juice and heat on medium until the mixture starts to boil. Reduce the heat to low, add the honey, and cook for about five minutes, mashing the whole time. Right at the end, cut up the cream cheese and add to the pan. Stir until the mixture is smooth. Let it cool to at least room temperature.

You can change ingredients, like the raisins, any way you want. Well-drained canned cherries are a good option.

Boursin Cheese

I used this a lot when I was competing and also at home for a variety of dishes. I especially like it in scrambled eggs. You can store for 2 weeks in the refrigerator, but it never lasts that long.

2 sticks unsalted butter, softened
2 (8-oz.) packages cream cheese, softened
1 Tbsp. minced garlic (I get mine from a jar)
1 Tbsp. Italian seasoning

Combine all ingredients in a medium bowl and mix well.

Chill at least 1 hour.

Makes 3 cups. You can easily cut this recipe in half.

Caramel Sauce

This one takes time, but it's much better than the store sauces. We use this for just about any dessert we have.

1 cup sugar
1 Tbsp. corn syrup
¼ cup water
½ cup heavy cream, warmed to about 110+ degrees
2 Tbsp. butter at room temperature
½ tsp. salt
1 tsp. vanilla

In a heavy saucepan, combine the sugar, syrup, and water until the sugar is completely moistened.

Begin cooking over high heat, stirring constantly, until the sugar dissolves and the syrup bubbles.

Stop stirring, turn the heat down to medium-high, and allow it to boil undisturbed until it starts to turn dark. Remove from the heat and carefully pour in the cream. It will boil like crazy.

Use a wooden spoon to stir the mixture until smooth. Stir in the butter and salt. Allow the sauce to cool for a few minutes and then gently stir in the vanilla.

Makes 1½ cups. Refrigerate the leftover sauce if you have any.

Coleslaw Dressing

You can shred a head of cabbage or just buy a big bag of coleslaw mix.

½ cup mayonnaise
¹⁄₃ cup sugar
¼ cup milk
¼ cup buttermilk
2½ Tbsp. lemon juice
1½ Tbsp. white vinegar
½ tsp. salt
¹⁄₈ tsp. pepper (15–20 turns on my pepper mill)
2 tsp. mustard powder

Whisk all ingredients together in a small mixing bowl and refrigerate for at least 1 hour.

This makes enough for one head of shredded cabbage. When you get ready to add this to the cabbage, whisk it again for 10 seconds. Sometimes we like to add a small can of chunk pineapple when we mix it, especially with BBQ pork dishes. Refrigerate the coleslaw for an hour or so to let the flavors meld.

Easiest Alfredo Sauce

1 Tbsp. minced garlic (I buy bottled minced garlic and sometimes smoked minced garlic)
1 package cream cheese, room temperature
8-oz. block Parmesan cheese, grated
1 stick butter, melted
½ cup whipping cream
milk

Add all of the ingredients to a medium saucepan and heat slowly, whisking constantly until smooth. If the sauce is too thick, stir in a little milk.

White Sauce

This sauce is one of the mother sauces and is used as the base for other sauces. For example, to make béchamel sauce, add 1 cup chicken broth in place of 1 cup milk.

¼ cup butter
¼ cup flour
1 small onion, diced
2 cups milk
salt and pepper taste

Heat butter in a medium saucepan. Add onions and cook until soft.

Mix in flour and simmer until the flour is totally incorporated. Stir until it starts to bubble.

Remove from heat and stir in milk. Return to heat and cook until thickened, stirring constantly. If it is too thick, add a little more milk.

Makes 2 cups

Other sauces you can make with this mother sauce

Cream sauce: Use cream in place of milk.

Cheese sauce: Add 8 oz. medium hard cheese, your choice.

Alfredo sauce: Add 1 cup fresh grated Parmesan cheese and 1 Tbsp. minced garlic.

Dijon sauce: Add 1 Tbsp. Dijon mustard and ¼ cup chopped mushrooms.

Béchamel sauce: Use 1 cup chicken broth in place of milk.

Florentine sauce: Add ½ cup finely chopped spinach.

Cake and Ice Cream Topping

10-inch oven
Serve over any non–fruit-flavored cake and/or ice cream

2 cups strawberries
2 cups cherries, fresh (if you can find them), frozen, or canned
2 Tbsp. butter
¾ cup sugar
1 Tbsp. cornstarch
1 Tbsp. lemon juice, either fresh or bottled

Combine the ingredients bring to a simmer and cook for 10 minutes or longer. The fruit will release natural pectin and the cornstarch will assist in thickening. Refrigerate for several hours.

My Fry Sauce

This sauce was made famous in Utah by the Arctic Circle drive-ins during the 1950s. This is the way I usually make it, although it sometimes changes a little.

2 Tbsp. Miracle Whip salad dressing
1 tsp. mustard powder
1 Tbsp. ketchup
1 tsp. ground black pepper

Mix the ingredients in a small bowl and serve with fries, hamburgers, etc.

Grandma's Brown Sugar Syrup

My very frugal Grandma made this for pancakes and French toast. She said it came from the Great Depression in the '30s. I always thought it was maple syrup. I didn't realize how easy this was to make until I was a teenager and she showed me how to make it. It tastes great!

1 cup brown sugar
1 cup boiling water
½ tsp. vanilla

Stir the brown sugar into the boiling water in the pan and let it dissolve. Simmer for 15 minutes until it starts to thicken a bit. Let it cool and stir in the vanilla.

Makes 2 cups

Quick Orange Glaze

Another easy summer topping, an orange glaze you can put together in two minutes.

1 cup powdered sugar
2 Tbsp. milk
juice and zest from one large orange
1 Tbsp. room temperature butter

Combine all of ingredients and whisk until smooth. If too thick, add a bit more milk until it is loose enough to drizzle. Serve over just about any baked dessert, warm or cooled—and, of course, with ice cream.

Pam's Shrimp Dip

We usually make this the night before a gathering and let it sit in the refrigerator overnight. I can eat it with a spoon.

8-oz. package cream cheese, softened
1 (10.5-oz.) can cream of mushroom soup
1 yellow onion, diced fine
1 package Knox unflavored gelatin
1 cup (8 oz.) mayonnaise
3 stalks celery, finely chopped
1 (5-oz.) can salad shrimp, drained and minced

Combine cream cheese, soup, and onion and heat until simmering; don't let it boil.

Dissolve gelatin in 2 tablespoons of hot water and add to the mixture.

Remove from heat and stir in the mayonnaise.

Add celery and shrimp. Chill for several hours and serve with your choice of crackers.

Vanilla Cream Sauce

1 cup apple juice, divided
4 oz. (1 stick) melted butter; nuke it for 20 seconds and then for 10 seconds
1 cup brown sugar
1 Tbsp. vanilla
1 cup whipping cream
1 Tbsp. cornstarch

In a small pot, mix together ¾ cup apple juice, butter, brown sugar, and cream. Heat it until it starts to bubble. Combine cornstarch with remaining apple juice. Add to pot and stir until thickened. Remove from heat and stir in vanilla. Serve warm or cooled over ice cream.

Vickie's Sweet and Sour Sauce

I started using this sauce during our early competition days. It is still one of my favorites.

1 cup ketchup
½ cup vinegar
¼ cup brown sugar
1 Tbsp. soy sauce
2 tsp. mustard powder
1 tsp. minced garlic
1 tsp. hot pepper sauce, optional (Sriracha, if you have it)
1 can diced tomatoes, drained
½ cup chopped canned pineapple
¼ cup cornstarch mixed with ¼ cup water, for thickening

Combine everything except the cornstarch in a big saucepan and heat until just boiling.

Stir the cornstarch and water one more time and add to the sauce, cooking until it thickens.

Serve over just about any meat where you want an Oriental flair.

Index

About the Author

Bruce Tracy started cooking for family and friends in his own backyard after receiving a Dutch oven from his wife Vickie for Father's Day in 1993. He soon began competing in cook-offs and won dozens of competitions, including the International Dutch Oven Society's World Championship in 2004. His first book, *Dutch Oven Baking*, is available online and in bookstores.

He doesn't compete these days, but instead uses his cooking and teaching background to teach Dutch oven cooks at all levels the joy of cooking in the venerable black pot.

Bruce and Vickie live in Ogden, Utah. (-:[>

0 26575 14207 5